C-3636   CAREER EXAMINATION SERIES

This is your
PASSBOOK for...

Insurance Adjuster

Test Preparation Study Guide
Questions & Answers

NATIONAL LEARNING CORPORATION®

COPYRIGHT NOTICE

This book is SOLELY intended for, is sold ONLY to, and its use is RESTRICTED to individual, bona fide applicants or candidates who qualify by virtue of having seriously filed applications for appropriate license, certificate, professional and/or promotional advancement, higher school matriculation, scholarship, or other legitimate requirements of education and/or governmental authorities.

This book is NOT intended for use, class instruction, tutoring, training, duplication, copying, reprinting, excerption, or adaptation, etc., by:

1) Other publishers
2) Proprietors and/or Instructors of "Coaching" and/or Preparatory Courses
3) Personnel and/or Training Divisions of commercial, industrial, and governmental organizations
4) Schools, colleges, or universities and/or their departments and staffs, including teachers and other personnel
5) Testing Agencies or Bureaus
6) Study groups which seek by the purchase of a single volume to copy and/or duplicate and/or adapt this material for use by the group as a whole without having purchased individual volumes for each of the members of the group
7) Et al.

Such persons would be in violation of appropriate Federal and State statutes.

PROVISION OF LICENSING AGREEMENTS – Recognized educational, commercial, industrial, and governmental institutions and organizations, and others legitimately engaged in educational pursuits, including training, testing, and measurement activities, may address request for a licensing agreement to the copyright owners, who will determine whether, and under what conditions, including fees and charges, the materials in this book may be used them. In other words, a licensing facility exists for the legitimate use of the material in this book on other than an individual basis. However, it is asseverated and affirmed here that the material in this book CANNOT be used without the receipt of the express permission of such a licensing agreement from the Publishers. Inquiries re licensing should be addressed to the company, attention rights and permissions department.

All rights reserved, including the right of reproduction in whole or in part, in any form or by any means, electronic or mechanical, including photocopying, recording, or by any information storage and retrieval system, without permission in writing from the Publisher.

Copyright © 2024 by
National Learning Corporation

212 Michael Drive, Syosset, NY 11791
(516) 921-8888 • www.passbooks.com
E-mail: info@passbooks.com

PASSBOOK® SERIES

THE *PASSBOOK® SERIES* has been created to prepare applicants and candidates for the ultimate academic battlefield – the examination room.

At some time in our lives, each and every one of us may be required to take an examination – for validation, matriculation, admission, qualification, registration, certification, or licensure.

Based on the assumption that every applicant or candidate has met the basic formal educational standards, has taken the required number of courses, and read the necessary texts, the *PASSBOOK® SERIES* furnishes the one special preparation which may assure passing with confidence, instead of failing with insecurity. Examination questions – together with answers – are furnished as the basic vehicle for study so that the mysteries of the examination and its compounding difficulties may be eliminated or diminished by a sure method.

This book is meant to help you pass your examination provided that you qualify and are serious in your objective.

The entire field is reviewed through the huge store of content information which is succinctly presented through a provocative and challenging approach – the question-and-answer method.

A climate of success is established by furnishing the correct answers at the end of each test.

You soon learn to recognize types of questions, forms of questions, and patterns of questioning. You may even begin to anticipate expected outcomes.

You perceive that many questions are repeated or adapted so that you can gain acute insights, which may enable you to score many sure points.

You learn how to confront new questions, or types of questions, and to attack them confidently and work out the correct answers.

You note objectives and emphases, and recognize pitfalls and dangers, so that you may make positive educational adjustments.

Moreover, you are kept fully informed in relation to new concepts, methods, practices, and directions in the field.

You discover that you are actually taking the examination all the time: you are preparing for the examination by "taking" an examination, not by reading extraneous and/or supererogatory textbooks.

In short, this PASSBOOK®, used directedly, should be an important factor in helping you to pass your test.

Section Four
Examination Contents for Public Adjuster and Independent Adjuster Tests

Public Adjuster (90 Questions)

Applicants for this type of license will be given an examination that includes 90 questions on claims adjusting for loss or damage to property of an insured in the State of New York from any of the risks enumerated in New York Insurance Law Sections 1113(a); 4 (fire), 5 (miscellaneous property insurance), 6 (water), 7 (burglary and theft), 8 (glass), 9 (boiler and machinery), 10 (elevator), and 20(B) and (C) (marine and inland marine insurance).

Public Adjuster's Ethics and Duties
Basic Principles of Law and Insurance
A. Indemnity
B. Friendly and hostile fires
C. Direct and consequential losses
D. Proximate cause
E. Law of Contracts
F. Representations and warranties
G. Material misrepresentations
H. Fraud and concealment
I. Physical hazards
J. Insurable interest
K. Waiver and estoppel
L. Binders
M. Cancellation of policies
N. Subrogation
O. Blanket and specific insurance
P. Primary and excess insurance

Loss Procedure
A. General
  1. Rights and obligations of insured after loss
  2. Negotiations with company or companies
  3. Establishment of liability under the contract
  4. Determination of value and loss
B. Building Losses
  1. Fundamentals of building and construction
  2. Estimates of repairs and rebuilding
  3. Depreciation
  4. Obsolescence
  5. Replacement cost
  6. Increased cost of construction required by municipal ordinances
C. Personal property and commodity losses
  1. Examination and checking of insured's records and merchandising methods
  2. Preparation of inventories of stock or other property in sight
  3. Determination of value of stock or other property burned out of sight or missing
  4. Salvage

New York Standard Fire Policy
(a comprehensive knowledge)

Forms and Clauses Attached to the Standard Fire Policy
A. Standard Dwelling forms
B. Farm form
C. Mortgagee clauses

Coverages Available in Connection With Fire Insurance
A. Extended coverages
B. Windstorm
C. Explosion
D. Sprinkler leakage
E. Water damage
F. Vandalism and malicious mischief
G. Consequential loss and damage assumption clauses
H. Profits and commissions and selling price clauses
I. Business interruption
J. Extra expense
K. Rent and rental value
L. Builder risk

VII. **Multiple Peril Policies and Forms**
  A. Special Multi-Peril policy
  B. Homeowners' policies

VIII. **Contribution and Apportionment**
  A. Loss problems under:
    1. Pro rata liability clause
    2. New York standard coinsurance clause
    3. Pro rata distribution clause
    4. Added clauses (such as extended coverages)
    5. Guiding principles

IX. **Insurance Law and Applicable Penal Laws**

Insurance Law Section		Penal Law
109	2126	Section 176
326	2127	176.05
1214	3404	
2101(g)	3405	
2102(a)(1)	3407	
2108	3408	
2110(a)(c)(e)(g)		
Regulation	10	

All Independent Adjusters

Adjuster's Ethics and Duties
A. To company
B. To insured
C. To other claimants

Insurance Laws and Applicable Penal Laws

Insurance Law Section		Penal Law
109	2126	Section 176
326	2127	176.05
1214	3404	
2101(g)	3405	
2102(a)(1)	3407	
2108	3408	
2110(a)(c)(e)(g)		
Regulation	25	

Accident and Health Adjuster (60 Questions)

I. **Individual Policies of Various Types**
(variation in benefits and provisions)
  A. The application
    1. Information required
    2. Necessity for same
  B. Insuring clause
  C. Benefits
    1. Accidental death, dismemberment, and loss of sight
    2. Principal and capital sum
    3. Loss of time:
       a. Total disability — variation of definition
       b. Partial disability — variation of benefits
    4. Elective indemnity; guaranteed minimum benefits for specified injuries
    5. Double indemnity
    6. Hospital and graduate nurse indemnities, surgical or medical benefits
       a. Hospital and graduate nurse indemnities
       b. Blanket medical expense reimbursement
       c. Surgical benefits
       d. Surgeon's fee for nondisabling injury
    7. Grace period
  D. Exceptions, exclusions, inclusions, and limitations; additional provisions

Examination Contents for Public Adjuster and Independent Adjuster Tests

- E. Miscellaneous provisions
    1. Effective date
    2. Renewals
    3. Assignment
    4. Change of beneficiary
    5. Lapse and reinstatement
    6. Cancellation (Pro rata; short rate)
- F. Uniform policy provisions
II. Medical Reimbursement
- A. Hospital expense
- B. Major medical
III. Group Disability Insurance
(knowledge of coverage and provisions)
- A. Group accident and/or health
- B. Hospital; surgical
- C. Blanket Accident and Health insurance
- D. Statutory disability insurance
    1. Benefits provided
    2. Claim procedure
IV. Medical Terms
(knowledge of medical terms and facts concerning injury and disease and the disabilities that they produce)
V. Information in Company Manuals, Types of Policies, Endorsements
- A. Variation as to policy forms
- B. General information, rules, and practices
- C. Classification of risks
- D. Effect of waiting period
- E. Coverages provided by endorsement
VI. General Principles and Terms
- A. Overinsurance
- B. Substandard risk
- C. Fraud
- D. Material misrepresentation
- E. Other insurance
- F. Other principles and terms
VIII. Adjustment Procedure
- A. Insured's compliance with policy provisions after loss (notice, proof of loss, etc.)
- B. Verification of policy coverage
- C. Investigation
    1. Statement of insured
    2. Report of doctor
    3. Medical examination
    4. Autopsy

Automobile Adjuster (60 Questions)

I. Automobile Physical Damage Coverages
- A. Comprehensive
- B. Collision or upset
- C. Combined additional coverages
- D. Towing and labor costs
- E. Personal effects (perils covered)
II. Automobile Liability Coverages
- A. Bodily injury
- B. Property damage
- C. Medical payments (optional)
- D. Defense, settlement, and supplementary expenses
III. Policy Provisions
(thorough knowledge of provisions contained in automobile policies)
- A. Insuring agreements
- B. Exclusions
    1. Use of automobile
    2. Causes and kinds of loss
    3. Assumed liability
    4. Employees and workers compensation
    5. Fraud, conversion, etc.
- C. Conditions
    1. Duties of:
        a. insured
        b. company
    2. Subrogation
    3. Other conditions of policy
IV. Classification of Automobile According to Use
- A. Private passenger
- B. Public
- C. Commercial
V. Manual Rules, Types and Scope of Coverage and Endorsements
- A. Physical damage
    1. Garagekeepers legal liability
    2. Dealers
- B. Liability
    1. Fleet
    2. Garage liability
    3. Named nonowner policy
    4. Schedule automobile liability policy
    5. Business auto policy
    6. Employers' nonownership liability
    7. Hired cars
    8. Protection against uninsured motorists
    9. New York Automobile Insurance Plan
- C. No-Fault Automobile Insurance
VI. Adjustment Procedure in Physical Damage Losses
- A. Verification of policy coverage
- B. Investigation and determining amount of damages
- C. Determining liability of company
- D. Type of interest
- E. Appraisal
VII. Adjustment Procedure in Liability Losses
- A. Verification of policy coverages
- B. Investigation of circumstances of accident
    1. Whether policy exclusion
    2. Diagram of location of accident
    3. Witnesses
    4. Statement of insured
- C. Insured's compliance with policy provisions after the loss (notice, suit, etc.)
- D. Releases
- E. Adjustment of claim with third party
VIII. Adjustment of Medical Payments Claims
IX. New York Motor Vehicle Financial Security Law
X. General Principles and Legal Terms
- A. Negligence
- B. Fraud
- C. Concealment and conversion
- D. Suit
- E. Waiver and estoppel
- F. Misrepresentations, declarations, and warranties
- G. Other insurance
XI. Medical Terms, Definitions

Aviation Adjuster (60 Questions)

I. Aviation Hull Coverages
- A. All risk (or comprehensive)
    1. Including crash
    2. Excluding crash
- B. Named peril policies
    1. Fire, lightning, and explosion
    2. Transportation
    3. Tornado, cyclone, and windstorm
    4. Theft, robbery, and pilferage
    5. Land damage
    6. Crash
    7. Mooring
- C. Application of deductibles
II. Aircraft Liability Coverages
- A. Bodily injury liability (excluding passengers)
- B. Property damage liability
- C. Passenger bodily injury liability
- D. Single limit liability policies
- E. Medical payments
    1. Including pilot
    2. Excluding pilot

Examination Contents for Public Adjuster and Independent Adjuster Tests

F. Admitted liability

Policy Provisions
A thorough knowledge of insuring agreements, exclusions, and conditions contained in Aviation Hull and Liability policies

Adjustment Procedure in Hull Losses
A. Verification of policy coverage
B. Determination whether policy provisions have been violated
C. Type of interest of insured
   1. Sole owner or other
   2. Mortgage with breach of warranty endorsement
D. Assured's compliance with policy provisions after loss (notice, proof of loss, protection of property, etc.)
E. Determination of amount of damages
F. Appraisal
G. Depreciation
H. Apportionment of duplicate policies
I. Company's options

Adjustment Procedure in Liability Losses
A. Verification of policy coverage
B. Investigation of circumstances of accident
C. Possible violation of policy provisions
D. Insured's compliance with policy provisions after loss (notice, suit, etc.)

Civil Aeronautics Administration and Its Regulations
A. Airworthiness certificate

General Principles and Definitions

In Flight	Conversion	Estoppel
Not in Flight	Concealment	Subrogation
Use of Airplane	Misrepresentation	Abandonment
Direct Loss	Fraud	Negligence
Consequential Loss	Warranties	General Average
Loss of Use	Waiver	Salvage
Proximate Cause		

V. **Adjustment Procedure in Bodily Injury Claims**
   A. Verification of policy coverage
   B. Investigation of circumstances of accident
      1. Whether policy exclusion
      2. Examination of location of accident
      3. Witnesses
      4. Statement of insured
      5. Statement of injured person
   C. Insured's compliance with policy provisions after loss (notice, suit, etc.)
   D. Releases
   E. Adjustment of claim with third party
   F. Suit
   G. Injuries to minor

VI. **Adjustment Procedure in Claims for Property Losses**
   A. Verification of policy coverage
   B. Investigating and determining amount of damages and company liability
   C. Type of insurable interest in damaged property
   D. Appraisal
   E. Proofs of Loss

VII. **Adjustment of Medical Payments Claims**

VIII. **Medical Terms, Common Injuries, and Occupational Diseases**

IX. **General Principles and Legal Terms**
   A. Negligence
   B. Fraud, concealment, conversion
   C. Suit
   D. Waiver and estoppel
   E. Subrogation
   F. Misrepresentations, declarations and warranties, and primary and excess insurance
   G. Other insurance
   H. Invitees, licensees, trespassers

Casualty Adjuster (60 Questions)

General Liability Policies — Knowledge of Coverage and Exclusions
A. Owners, Landlords, and Tenants
B. Manufacturers and Contractors
C. Elevator
D. Contractual
E. Protective
F. Products
G. Comprehensive General
H. Comprehensive Personal
I. Storekeepers
J. Medical payments in connection with various liability forms
K. Druggists
L. Miscellaneous Professional

Workers Compensation & Employer's Liability
A. New York State Workers Compensation Act
B. Standard policy provisions
C. Occupations covered by law
D. Compensable injuries
E. Benefits for injuries, disability, or death (Schedule Awards)
F. Disease coverage
G. Procedure and forms required by Workers Compensation Board

Miscellaneous Casualty Lines
A. Glass
   1. Types insured
   2. Extent of coverage
   3. Endorsements
B. Boiler and Machinery
   1. Basic policy; required and optional coverages; limits
   2. Consequential (indirect) Damage, Time Element coverages

Burglary, Robbery, Theft
A. Personal Theft and Broad Form Personal Theft
B. Storekeepers burglary and robbery and Broad Form storekeepers policy
C. Interior, messenger, and paymaster robbery
D. Broad Form Money and Securities
E. Safe burglary
F. Mercantile open stock burglary
G. Miscellaneous burglary, robbery, and crime policies

Fidelity and Surety Adjuster (60 Questions)

I. **Basic Principles**
   A. Collateral security
   B. Indemnity agreements
   C. Co-surety
   D. Joint control
   E. Misrepresentations
   F. Primary and excess coverage
   G. Subrogation

II. **Types of Bonds**
   (a thorough knowledge of)
   A. Fidelity
      1. Individual and Schedule
      2. Blanket
         a. Blanket Position
         b. Commercial Blanket
         c. Bankers and Brokers Blanket
         d. Public Employees Blanket
         e. Comprehensive Dishonesty, Destruction, and Disappearance
   B. Surety
      1. Contract
         a. Bid
         b. Construction
         c. Maintenance
         d. Performance
         e. Supply
      2. Depositors Forgery
      3. Court bonds
         a. Probate
         b. Litigation
      4. License and Permit
         a. Lost Securities
         b. Public Officials

Examination Contents for Public Adjuster and Independent Adjuster Tests

Fire Adjuster (60 Questions)

I. **Basic Principles of Law and Insurance**
   A. Indemnity
   B. Friendly and hostile fires
   C. Direct and consequential losses
   D. Proximate cause
   E. Law of contracts
   F. Representations and warranties
   G. Fraud and concealment
   H. Insurable interest
   I. Waiver and estoppel
   J. Binders
   K. Cancellation of policies
   L. Subrogation
   M. Blanket and specific insurance

II. **Loss Procedure**
   A. General
      1. Rights and obligations of insured
      2. Negotiations with company or companies
      3. Establishment of liability under policy
      4. Increased cost of construction
   B. Building Losses
      1. Fundamentals of building construction
      2. Estimates of repairs and rebuilding
      3. Depreciation, obsolescence, and replacement costs
      4. Increased cost of construction
   C. Personal property and commodity losses
      1. Examination and checking of insured's records and merchandising methods
      2. Preparation of inventories of stock or other property in sight
      3. Determination of value of stock or other property burned out of sight or missing
      4. Salvage

III. **New York Standard Fire Policy**
   (a comprehensive knowledge)

IV. **Forms and Clauses Attached to the Standard Fire Policy**
   A. Dwelling property form
   B. Other property forms
   C. Mortgages clauses

V. **Coverages Available in Connection With Fire Insurance**
   A. Extended coverages
   B. Sprinkler leakage
   C. Water damage
   D. Vandalism and malicious mischief
   E. Consequential loss and damage assumption clauses
   F. Selling price clauses
   G. Business interruption and earnings insurance
   H. Extra expense
   I. Rent and rental value
   J. Builders risk

VI. **Multiple Peril Policies and Forms**
   A. Homeowners policies
   B. Commercial property forms

VII. **Contribution and Apportionment**
   A. Loss problems under:
      1. Pro rata liability clause
      2. New York Standard Coinsurance clause
      3. Pro rata distribution clause
      4. Guiding principles

Inland Marine Adjuster (60 Questions)

I. **General Principles**
   A. Nationwide Definition of Inland Marine insurance
   B. Declarations and warranties
   C. Waiver and estoppel
   D. All-risk vs. named perils
   E. Reporting form policies
   F. Schedule policies
   G. Clauses (pair and set, sue and labor, etc.)
   H. Material misrepresentations
   I. Subrogation
   J. Agreements of Guiding Principles to cases of overlapping coverages

II. **Loss Procedure**
   A. Rights and obligations of the insured after a loss
   B. Establishment of liability
   C. Negotiations with company or companies
   D. Determination of value and loss
   E. Primary and excess insurance
   F. F.O.B. shipments

III. **Transportation Policies**
   (Provisions and Exclusions)
   A. Annual Transportation policies
   B. Trip Transit
   C. Motor Truck Cargo; Owner form, Truckers form
   D. I.C.C. Endorsement — requirements, effect on liability
   E. Special Transportation forms, such as Department Store Floater Garment Contractors Floater, etc.

IV. **Commercial Floaters**
   (Provisions and Exclusions)
   A. Bailees Customers policies, such as Furriers Customers, Laundry and Dry Cleaners, etc.
   B. Dealers policies

V. **Personal Floaters**
   (Provisions and Exclusions)
   A. Personal Property floater
   B. Personal Effects floater
   C. Personal Articles (Jewelry, Furs, etc.)
   (All forms of personal floaters should be studied)

General Adjuster (120 Questions)

Applicants for this type of license will be given an examination that includes questions on the adjusting of all of the following types of loss: Accident and Health, Automobile, Aviation, Casualty, Fidelity and Surety, Fire, and Inland Marine. They should be familiar with the material in each of the seven preceding Independent Adjuster outlines in this Section.

Automobile Damage or Theft Appraisals Adjuster (Only) (50 Questions)

The Independent Adjuster, Automobile Damage or Theft Appraisals, shall have authority to appraise and adjust all claims arising under automobile physical damage coverages. For claims arising under property damage liability insurance policies, the authority of any adjuster licensed under this subdivision is limited to appraisal of damage to automobiles.

Set forth in the following outline are the principal topics which examinations for licenses as Independent Adjuster, Automobile Damage or Theft Appraisals, will be based. It is to be understood, however, that questions based on additional topics may be used in such examinations, should it prove to be advisable to do so.

I. **Duties**
   A. To the insured
   B. To the company

II. **Automobile Physical Damage**
   A. Comprehensive
      1. Actual cash value and stated amount
      2. Deductibles
      3. Hazards covered
   B. Collision Insurance
      1. Hazards covered

Examination Contents for Public Adjuster and Independent Adjuster Tests

    2. Deductibles
C. Other
    1. Fire and theft
    2. Towing and labor

Adjustment Procedure
A. Verification of coverage
B. Investigating and determining amount of damages
C. Insurance company's liability
D. Type of interest
    1. Sole owner
    2. Financed auto, other interest
E. Appraisal
F. Insured's duties — notice of accident — cooperation with company

Statutory
A. N.Y. Financial Security Law
B. N.Y. Automobile Insurance Plan

Appraisals
A. General questions relative to appraisal of automobile physical damage including but not limited to the following:
    1. Industry terminology
        a. Overlap labor
        b. Included operation
        c. "R" & "R"
        d. Overhaul
    2. Identification of Vehicle

    3. Parts of an automobile
        a. Body parts
        b. Suspension systems
        c. Transmission
        d. Air conditioners
        e. Tires
        f. Moulding, ornamentation, decals, or overlays
        g. Relationship of one part to another
        h. Types of damage
        i. Repair of replacement of damaged components
        j. Unique design or engineering features of certain automobiles
    4. Painting operations
        a. Single color
        b. Two tone
        c. Adjacent panels

VI. **Sections of Law**
Insurance Law

Section	109	2108
	326	2110(a)(c)(e)(g)
	2101(g)	2126
	2102(a)(1)	2127
Regulation	25	
Regulation	64	

HOW TO TAKE A TEST

I. YOU MUST PASS AN EXAMINATION

A. *WHAT EVERY CANDIDATE SHOULD KNOW*

Examination applicants often ask us for help in preparing for the written test. What can I study in advance? What kinds of questions will be asked? How will the test be given? How will the papers be graded?

As an applicant for a civil service examination, you may be wondering about some of these things. Our purpose here is to suggest effective methods of advance study and to describe civil service examinations.

Your chances for success on this examination can be increased if you know how to prepare. Those "pre-examination jitters" can be reduced if you know what to expect. You can even experience an adventure in good citizenship if you know why civil service exams are given.

B. *WHY ARE CIVIL SERVICE EXAMINATIONS GIVEN?*

Civil service examinations are important to you in two ways. As a citizen, you want public jobs filled by employees who know how to do their work. As a job seeker, you want a fair chance to compete for that job on an equal footing with other candidates. The best-known means of accomplishing this two-fold goal is the competitive examination.

Exams are widely publicized throughout the nation. They may be administered for jobs in federal, state, city, municipal, town or village governments or agencies.

Any citizen may apply, with some limitations, such as the age or residence of applicants. Your experience and education may be reviewed to see whether you meet the requirements for the particular examination. When these requirements exist, they are reasonable and applied consistently to all applicants. Thus, a competitive examination may cause you some uneasiness now, but it is your privilege and safeguard.

C. *HOW ARE CIVIL SERVICE EXAMS DEVELOPED?*

Examinations are carefully written by trained technicians who are specialists in the field known as "psychological measurement," in consultation with recognized authorities in the field of work that the test will cover. These experts recommend the subject matter areas or skills to be tested; only those knowledges or skills important to your success on the job are included. The most reliable books and source materials available are used as references. Together, the experts and technicians judge the difficulty level of the questions.

Test technicians know how to phrase questions so that the problem is clearly stated. Their ethics do not permit "trick" or "catch" questions. Questions may have been tried out on sample groups, or subjected to statistical analysis, to determine their usefulness.

Written tests are often used in combination with performance tests, ratings of training and experience, and oral interviews. All of these measures combine to form the best-known means of finding the right person for the right job.

II. HOW TO PASS THE WRITTEN TEST

A. NATURE OF THE EXAMINATION

To prepare intelligently for civil service examinations, you should know how they differ from school examinations you have taken. In school you were assigned certain definite pages to read or subjects to cover. The examination questions were quite detailed and usually emphasized memory. Civil service exams, on the other hand, try to discover your present ability to perform the duties of a position, plus your potentiality to learn these duties. In other words, a civil service exam attempts to predict how successful you will be. Questions cover such a broad area that they cannot be as minute and detailed as school exam questions.

In the public service similar kinds of work, or positions, are grouped together in one "class." This process is known as *position-classification*. All the positions in a class are paid according to the salary range for that class. One class title covers all of these positions, and they are all tested by the same examination.

B. FOUR BASIC STEPS

1) Study the announcement

How, then, can you know what subjects to study? Our best answer is: "Learn as much as possible about the class of positions for which you've applied." The exam will test the knowledge, skills and abilities needed to do the work.

Your most valuable source of information about the position you want is the official exam announcement. This announcement lists the training and experience qualifications. Check these standards and apply only if you come reasonably close to meeting them.

The brief description of the position in the examination announcement offers some clues to the subjects which will be tested. Think about the job itself. Review the duties in your mind. Can you perform them, or are there some in which you are rusty? Fill in the blank spots in your preparation.

Many jurisdictions preview the written test in the exam announcement by including a section called "Knowledge and Abilities Required," "Scope of the Examination," or some similar heading. Here you will find out specifically what fields will be tested.

2) Review your own background

Once you learn in general what the position is all about, and what you need to know to do the work, ask yourself which subjects you already know fairly well and which need improvement. You may wonder whether to concentrate on improving your strong areas or on building some background in your fields of weakness. When the announcement has specified "some knowledge" or "considerable knowledge," or has used adjectives like "beginning principles of..." or "advanced ... methods," you can get a clue as to the number and difficulty of questions to be asked in any given field. More questions, and hence broader coverage, would be included for those subjects which are more important in the work. Now weigh your strengths and weaknesses against the job requirements and prepare accordingly.

3) Determine the level of the position

Another way to tell how intensively you should prepare is to understand the level of the job for which you are applying. Is it the entering level? In other words, is this the position in which beginners in a field of work are hired? Or is it an intermediate or advanced level? Sometimes this is indicated by such words as "Junior" or "Senior" in the class title. Other jurisdictions use Roman numerals to designate the level – Clerk I, Clerk II, for example. The word "Supervisor" sometimes appears in the title. If the level is not indicated by the title, check the description of duties. Will you be working under very close supervision, or will you have responsibility for independent decisions in this work?

4) Choose appropriate study materials

Now that you know the subjects to be examined and the relative amount of each subject to be covered, you can choose suitable study materials. For beginning level jobs, or even advanced ones, if you have a pronounced weakness in some aspect of your training, read a modern, standard textbook in that field. Be sure it is up to date and has general coverage. Such books are normally available at your library, and the librarian will be glad to help you locate one. For entry-level positions, questions of appropriate difficulty are chosen – neither highly advanced questions, nor those too simple. Such questions require careful thought but not advanced training.

If the position for which you are applying is technical or advanced, you will read more advanced, specialized material. If you are already familiar with the basic principles of your field, elementary textbooks would waste your time. Concentrate on advanced textbooks and technical periodicals. Think through the concepts and review difficult problems in your field.

These are all general sources. You can get more ideas on your own initiative, following these leads. For example, training manuals and publications of the government agency which employs workers in your field can be useful, particularly for technical and professional positions. A letter or visit to the government department involved may result in more specific study suggestions, and certainly will provide you with a more definite idea of the exact nature of the position you are seeking.

III. KINDS OF TESTS

Tests are used for purposes other than measuring knowledge and ability to perform specified duties. For some positions, it is equally important to test ability to make adjustments to new situations or to profit from training. In others, basic mental abilities not dependent on information are essential. Questions which test these things may not appear as pertinent to the duties of the position as those which test for knowledge and information. Yet they are often highly important parts of a fair examination. For very general questions, it is almost impossible to help you direct your study efforts. What we can do is to point out some of the more common of these general abilities needed in public service positions and describe some typical questions.

1) General information

Broad, general information has been found useful for predicting job success in some kinds of work. This is tested in a variety of ways, from vocabulary lists to questions about current events. Basic background in some field of work, such as sociology or economics, may be sampled in a group of questions. Often these are principles which have become familiar to most persons through exposure rather than through formal training. It is difficult to advise you how to study for these questions; being alert to the world around you is our best suggestion.

2) Verbal ability

An example of an ability needed in many positions is verbal or language ability. Verbal ability is, in brief, the ability to use and understand words. Vocabulary and grammar tests are typical measures of this ability. Reading comprehension or paragraph interpretation questions are common in many kinds of civil service tests. You are given a paragraph of written material and asked to find its central meaning.

3) Numerical ability
Number skills can be tested by the familiar arithmetic problem, by checking paired lists of numbers to see which are alike and which are different, or by interpreting charts and graphs. In the latter test, a graph may be printed in the test booklet which you are asked to use as the basis for answering questions.

4) Observation
A popular test for law-enforcement positions is the observation test. A picture is shown to you for several minutes, then taken away. Questions about the picture test your ability to observe both details and larger elements.

5) Following directions
In many positions in the public service, the employee must be able to carry out written instructions dependably and accurately. You may be given a chart with several columns, each column listing a variety of information. The questions require you to carry out directions involving the information given in the chart.

6) Skills and aptitudes
Performance tests effectively measure some manual skills and aptitudes. When the skill is one in which you are trained, such as typing or shorthand, you can practice. These tests are often very much like those given in business school or high school courses. For many of the other skills and aptitudes, however, no short-time preparation can be made. Skills and abilities natural to you or that you have developed throughout your lifetime are being tested.

Many of the general questions just described provide all the data needed to answer the questions and ask you to use your reasoning ability to find the answers. Your best preparation for these tests, as well as for tests of facts and ideas, is to be at your physical and mental best. You, no doubt, have your own methods of getting into an exam-taking mood and keeping "in shape." The next section lists some ideas on this subject.

IV. KINDS OF QUESTIONS

Only rarely is the "essay" question, which you answer in narrative form, used in civil service tests. Civil service tests are usually of the short-answer type. Full instructions for answering these questions will be given to you at the examination. But in case this is your first experience with short-answer questions and separate answer sheets, here is what you need to know:

1) **Multiple-choice Questions**
Most popular of the short-answer questions is the "multiple choice" or "best answer" question. It can be used, for example, to test for factual knowledge, ability to solve problems or judgment in meeting situations found at work.
A multiple-choice question is normally one of three types—
- It can begin with an incomplete statement followed by several possible endings. You are to find the one ending which *best* completes the statement, although some of the others may not be entirely wrong.
- It can also be a complete statement in the form of a question which is answered by choosing one of the statements listed.

- It can be in the form of a problem – again you select the best answer.

Here is an example of a multiple-choice question with a discussion which should give you some clues as to the method for choosing the right answer:

When an employee has a complaint about his assignment, the action which will *best* help him overcome his difficulty is to
   A. discuss his difficulty with his coworkers
   B. take the problem to the head of the organization
   C. take the problem to the person who gave him the assignment
   D. say nothing to anyone about his complaint

In answering this question, you should study each of the choices to find which is best. Consider choice "A" – Certainly an employee may discuss his complaint with fellow employees, but no change or improvement can result, and the complaint remains unresolved. Choice "B" is a poor choice since the head of the organization probably does not know what assignment you have been given, and taking your problem to him is known as "going over the head" of the supervisor. The supervisor, or person who made the assignment, is the person who can clarify it or correct any injustice. Choice "C" is, therefore, correct. To say nothing, as in choice "D," is unwise. Supervisors have and interest in knowing the problems employees are facing, and the employee is seeking a solution to his problem.

2) True/False Questions

The "true/false" or "right/wrong" form of question is sometimes used. Here a complete statement is given. Your job is to decide whether the statement is right or wrong.

SAMPLE: A roaming cell-phone call to a nearby city costs less than a non-roaming call to a distant city.

This statement is wrong, or false, since roaming calls are more expensive.

This is not a complete list of all possible question forms, although most of the others are variations of these common types. You will always get complete directions for answering questions. Be sure you understand *how* to mark your answers – ask questions until you do.

V. RECORDING YOUR ANSWERS

Computer terminals are used more and more today for many different kinds of exams.

For an examination with very few applicants, you may be told to record your answers in the test booklet itself. Separate answer sheets are much more common. If this separate answer sheet is to be scored by machine – and this is often the case – it is highly important that you mark your answers correctly in order to get credit.

An electronic scoring machine is often used in civil service offices because of the speed with which papers can be scored. Machine-scored answer sheets must be marked with a pencil, which will be given to you. This pencil has a high graphite content which responds to the electronic scoring machine. As a matter of fact, stray dots may register as answers, so do not let your pencil rest on the answer sheet while you are pondering the correct answer. Also, if your pencil lead breaks or is otherwise defective, ask for another.

Since the answer sheet will be dropped in a slot in the scoring machine, be careful not to bend the corners or get the paper crumpled.

The answer sheet normally has five vertical columns of numbers, with 30 numbers to a column. These numbers correspond to the question numbers in your test booklet. After each number, going across the page are four or five pairs of dotted lines. These short dotted lines have small letters or numbers above them. The first two pairs may also have a "T" or "F" above the letters. This indicates that the first two pairs only are to be used if the questions are of the true-false type. If the questions are multiple choice, disregard the "T" and "F" and pay attention only to the small letters or numbers.

Answer your questions in the manner of the sample that follows:

32. The largest city in the United States is
    A. Washington, D.C.
    B. New York City
    C. Chicago
    D. Detroit
    E. San Francisco

1) Choose the answer you think is best. (New York City is the largest, so "B" is correct.)
2) Find the row of dotted lines numbered the same as the question you are answering. (Find row number 32)
3) Find the pair of dotted lines corresponding to the answer. (Find the pair of lines under the mark "B.")
4) Make a solid black mark between the dotted lines.

VI. BEFORE THE TEST

Common sense will help you find procedures to follow to get ready for an examination. Too many of us, however, overlook these sensible measures. Indeed, nervousness and fatigue have been found to be the most serious reasons why applicants fail to do their best on civil service tests. Here is a list of reminders:

- Begin your preparation early – Don't wait until the last minute to go scurrying around for books and materials or to find out what the position is all about.
- Prepare continuously – An hour a night for a week is better than an all-night cram session. This has been definitely established. What is more, a night a week for a month will return better dividends than crowding your study into a shorter period of time.
- Locate the place of the exam – You have been sent a notice telling you when and where to report for the examination. If the location is in a different town or otherwise unfamiliar to you, it would be well to inquire the best route and learn something about the building.
- Relax the night before the test – Allow your mind to rest. Do not study at all that night. Plan some mild recreation or diversion; then go to bed early and get a good night's sleep.
- Get up early enough to make a leisurely trip to the place for the test – This way unforeseen events, traffic snarls, unfamiliar buildings, etc. will not upset you.
- Dress comfortably – A written test is not a fashion show. You will be known by number and not by name, so wear something comfortable.

- Leave excess paraphernalia at home – Shopping bags and odd bundles will get in your way. You need bring only the items mentioned in the official notice you received; usually everything you need is provided. Do not bring reference books to the exam. They will only confuse those last minutes and be taken away from you when in the test room.
- Arrive somewhat ahead of time – If because of transportation schedules you must get there very early, bring a newspaper or magazine to take your mind off yourself while waiting.
- Locate the examination room – When you have found the proper room, you will be directed to the seat or part of the room where you will sit. Sometimes you are given a sheet of instructions to read while you are waiting. Do not fill out any forms until you are told to do so; just read them and be prepared.
- Relax and prepare to listen to the instructions
- If you have any physical problem that may keep you from doing your best, be sure to tell the test administrator. If you are sick or in poor health, you really cannot do your best on the exam. You can come back and take the test some other time.

VII. AT THE TEST

The day of the test is here and you have the test booklet in your hand. The temptation to get going is very strong. Caution! There is more to success than knowing the right answers. You must know how to identify your papers and understand variations in the type of short-answer question used in this particular examination. Follow these suggestions for maximum results from your efforts:

1) Cooperate with the monitor

The test administrator has a duty to create a situation in which you can be as much at ease as possible. He will give instructions, tell you when to begin, check to see that you are marking your answer sheet correctly, and so on. He is not there to guard you, although he will see that your competitors do not take unfair advantage. He wants to help you do your best.

2) Listen to all instructions

Don't jump the gun! Wait until you understand all directions. In most civil service tests you get more time than you need to answer the questions. So don't be in a hurry. Read each word of instructions until you clearly understand the meaning. Study the examples, listen to all announcements and follow directions. Ask questions if you do not understand what to do.

3) Identify your papers

Civil service exams are usually identified by number only. You will be assigned a number; you must not put your name on your test papers. Be sure to copy your number correctly. Since more than one exam may be given, copy your exact examination title.

4) Plan your time

Unless you are told that a test is a "speed" or "rate of work" test, speed itself is usually not important. Time enough to answer all the questions will be provided, but this does not mean that you have all day. An overall time limit has been set. Divide the total time (in minutes) by the number of questions to determine the approximate time you have for each question.

5) Do not linger over difficult questions

If you come across a difficult question, mark it with a paper clip (useful to have along) and come back to it when you have been through the booklet. One caution if you do this – be sure to skip a number on your answer sheet as well. Check often to be sure that you have not lost your place and that you are marking in the row numbered the same as the question you are answering.

6) Read the questions

Be sure you know what the question asks! Many capable people are unsuccessful because they failed to *read* the questions correctly.

7) Answer all questions

Unless you have been instructed that a penalty will be deducted for incorrect answers, it is better to guess than to omit a question.

8) Speed tests

It is often better NOT to guess on speed tests. It has been found that on timed tests people are tempted to spend the last few seconds before time is called in marking answers at random – without even reading them – in the hope of picking up a few extra points. To discourage this practice, the instructions may warn you that your score will be "corrected" for guessing. That is, a penalty will be applied. The incorrect answers will be deducted from the correct ones, or some other penalty formula will be used.

9) Review your answers

If you finish before time is called, go back to the questions you guessed or omitted to give them further thought. Review other answers if you have time.

10) Return your test materials

If you are ready to leave before others have finished or time is called, take ALL your materials to the monitor and leave quietly. Never take any test material with you. The monitor can discover whose papers are not complete, and taking a test booklet may be grounds for disqualification.

VIII. EXAMINATION TECHNIQUES

1) Read the general instructions carefully. These are usually printed on the first page of the exam booklet. As a rule, these instructions refer to the timing of the examination; the fact that you should not start work until the signal and must stop work at a signal, etc. If there are any *special* instructions, such as a choice of questions to be answered, make sure that you note this instruction carefully.

2) When you are ready to start work on the examination, that is as soon as the signal has been given, read the instructions to each question booklet, underline any key words or phrases, such as *least, best, outline, describe* and the like. In this way you will tend to answer as requested rather than discover on reviewing your paper that you *listed without describing*, that you selected the *worst* choice rather than the *best* choice, etc.

3) If the examination is of the objective or multiple-choice type – that is, each question will also give a series of possible answers: A, B, C or D, and you are called upon to select the best answer and write the letter next to that answer on your answer paper – it is advisable to start answering each question in turn. There may be anywhere from 50 to 100 such questions in the three or four hours allotted and you can see how much time would be taken if you read through all the questions before beginning to answer any. Furthermore, if you come across a question or group of questions which you know would be difficult to answer, it would undoubtedly affect your handling of all the other questions.

4) If the examination is of the essay type and contains but a few questions, it is a moot point as to whether you should read all the questions before starting to answer any one. Of course, if you are given a choice – say five out of seven and the like – then it is essential to read all the questions so you can eliminate the two that are most difficult. If, however, you are asked to answer all the questions, there may be danger in trying to answer the easiest one first because you may find that you will spend too much time on it. The best technique is to answer the first question, then proceed to the second, etc.

5) Time your answers. Before the exam begins, write down the time it started, then add the time allowed for the examination and write down the time it must be completed, then divide the time available somewhat as follows:
    - If 3-1/2 hours are allowed, that would be 210 minutes. If you have 80 objective-type questions, that would be an average of 2-1/2 minutes per question. Allow yourself no more than 2 minutes per question, or a total of 160 minutes, which will permit about 50 minutes to review.
    - If for the time allotment of 210 minutes there are 7 essay questions to answer, that would average about 30 minutes a question. Give yourself only 25 minutes per question so that you have about 35 minutes to review.

6) The most important instruction is to *read each question* and make sure you know what is wanted. The second most important instruction is to *time yourself properly* so that you answer every question. The third most important instruction is to *answer every question*. Guess if you have to but include something for each question. Remember that you will receive no credit for a blank and will probably receive some credit if you write something in answer to an essay question. If you guess a letter – say "B" for a multiple-choice question – you may have guessed right. If you leave a blank as an answer to a multiple-choice question, the examiners may respect your feelings but it will not add a point to your score. Some exams may penalize you for wrong answers, so in such cases *only*, you may not want to guess unless you have some basis for your answer.

7) Suggestions
    a. Objective-type questions
        1. Examine the question booklet for proper sequence of pages and questions
        2. Read all instructions carefully
        3. Skip any question which seems too difficult; return to it after all other questions have been answered
        4. Apportion your time properly; do not spend too much time on any single question or group of questions

5. Note and underline key words – *all, most, fewest, least, best, worst, same, opposite,* etc.
6. Pay particular attention to negatives
7. Note unusual option, e.g., unduly long, short, complex, different or similar in content to the body of the question
8. Observe the use of "hedging" words – *probably, may, most likely,* etc.
9. Make sure that your answer is put next to the same number as the question
10. Do not second-guess unless you have good reason to believe the second answer is definitely more correct
11. Cross out original answer if you decide another answer is more accurate; do not erase until you are ready to hand your paper in
12. Answer all questions; guess unless instructed otherwise
13. Leave time for review

  b. Essay questions
    1. Read each question carefully
    2. Determine exactly what is wanted. Underline key words or phrases.
    3. Decide on outline or paragraph answer
    4. Include many different points and elements unless asked to develop any one or two points or elements
    5. Show impartiality by giving pros and cons unless directed to select one side only
    6. Make and write down any assumptions you find necessary to answer the questions
    7. Watch your English, grammar, punctuation and choice of words
    8. Time your answers; don't crowd material

8) Answering the essay question

Most essay questions can be answered by framing the specific response around several key words or ideas. Here are a few such key words or ideas:

M's: manpower, materials, methods, money, management
P's: purpose, program, policy, plan, procedure, practice, problems, pitfalls, personnel, public relations

  a. Six basic steps in handling problems:
    1. Preliminary plan and background development
    2. Collect information, data and facts
    3. Analyze and interpret information, data and facts
    4. Analyze and develop solutions as well as make recommendations
    5. Prepare report and sell recommendations
    6. Install recommendations and follow up effectiveness

  b. Pitfalls to avoid
    1. *Taking things for granted* – A statement of the situation does not necessarily imply that each of the elements is necessarily true; for example, a complaint may be invalid and biased so that all that can be taken for granted is that a complaint has been registered

2. *Considering only one side of a situation* – Wherever possible, indicate several alternatives and then point out the reasons you selected the best one
3. *Failing to indicate follow up* – Whenever your answer indicates action on your part, make certain that you will take proper follow-up action to see how successful your recommendations, procedures or actions turn out to be
4. *Taking too long in answering any single question* – Remember to time your answers properly

IX. AFTER THE TEST

Scoring procedures differ in detail among civil service jurisdictions although the general principles are the same. Whether the papers are hand-scored or graded by machine we have described, they are nearly always graded by number. That is, the person who marks the paper knows only the number – never the name – of the applicant. Not until all the papers have been graded will they be matched with names. If other tests, such as training and experience or oral interview ratings have been given, scores will be combined. Different parts of the examination usually have different weights. For example, the written test might count 60 percent of the final grade, and a rating of training and experience 40 percent. In many jurisdictions, veterans will have a certain number of points added to their grades.

After the final grade has been determined, the names are placed in grade order and an eligible list is established. There are various methods for resolving ties between those who get the same final grade – probably the most common is to place first the name of the person whose application was received first. Job offers are made from the eligible list in the order the names appear on it. You will be notified of your grade and your rank as soon as all these computations have been made. This will be done as rapidly as possible.

People who are found to meet the requirements in the announcement are called "eligibles." Their names are put on a list of eligible candidates. An eligible's chances of getting a job depend on how high he stands on this list and how fast agencies are filling jobs from the list.

When a job is to be filled from a list of eligibles, the agency asks for the names of people on the list of eligibles for that job. When the civil service commission receives this request, it sends to the agency the names of the three people highest on this list. Or, if the job to be filled has specialized requirements, the office sends the agency the names of the top three persons who meet these requirements from the general list.

The appointing officer makes a choice from among the three people whose names were sent to him. If the selected person accepts the appointment, the names of the others are put back on the list to be considered for future openings.

That is the rule in hiring from all kinds of eligible lists, whether they are for typist, carpenter, chemist, or something else. For every vacancy, the appointing officer has his choice of any one of the top three eligibles on the list. This explains why the person whose name is on top of the list sometimes does not get an appointment when some of the persons lower on the list do. If the appointing officer chooses the second or third eligible, the No. 1 eligible does not get a job at once, but stays on the list until he is appointed or the list is terminated.

X. HOW TO PASS THE INTERVIEW TEST

The examination for which you applied requires an oral interview test. You have already taken the written test and you are now being called for the interview test – the final part of the formal examination.

You may think that it is not possible to prepare for an interview test and that there are no procedures to follow during an interview. Our purpose is to point out some things you can do in advance that will help you and some good rules to follow and pitfalls to avoid while you are being interviewed.

What is an interview supposed to test?

The written examination is designed to test the technical knowledge and competence of the candidate; the oral is designed to evaluate intangible qualities, not readily measured otherwise, and to establish a list showing the relative fitness of each candidate – as measured against his competitors – for the position sought. Scoring is not on the basis of "right" and "wrong," but on a sliding scale of values ranging from "not passable" to "outstanding." As a matter of fact, it is possible to achieve a relatively low score without a single "incorrect" answer because of evident weakness in the qualities being measured.

Occasionally, an examination may consist entirely of an oral test – either an individual or a group oral. In such cases, information is sought concerning the technical knowledges and abilities of the candidate, since there has been no written examination for this purpose. More commonly, however, an oral test is used to supplement a written examination.

Who conducts interviews?

The composition of oral boards varies among different jurisdictions. In nearly all, a representative of the personnel department serves as chairman. One of the members of the board may be a representative of the department in which the candidate would work. In some cases, "outside experts" are used, and, frequently, a businessman or some other representative of the general public is asked to serve. Labor and management or other special groups may be represented. The aim is to secure the services of experts in the appropriate field.

However the board is composed, it is a good idea (and not at all improper or unethical) to ascertain in advance of the interview who the members are and what groups they represent. When you are introduced to them, you will have some idea of their backgrounds and interests, and at least you will not stutter and stammer over their names.

What should be done before the interview?

While knowledge about the board members is useful and takes some of the surprise element out of the interview, there is other preparation which is more substantive. It *is* possible to prepare for an oral interview – in several ways:

1) Keep a copy of your application and review it carefully before the interview

This may be the only document before the oral board, and the starting point of the interview. Know what education and experience you have listed there, and the sequence and dates of all of it. Sometimes the board will ask you to review the highlights of your experience for them; you should not have to hem and haw doing it.

2) Study the class specification and the examination announcement

Usually, the oral board has one or both of these to guide them. The qualities, characteristics or knowledges required by the position sought are stated in these documents. They offer valuable clues as to the nature of the oral interview. For example, if the job involves supervisory responsibilities, the announcement will usually indicate that knowledge of modern supervisory methods and the qualifications of the candidate as a supervisor will be tested. If so, you can expect such questions, frequently in the form of a hypothetical situation which you are expected to solve. NEVER go into an oral without knowledge of the duties and responsibilities of the job you seek.

3) Think through each qualification required

Try to visualize the kind of questions you would ask if you were a board member. How well could you answer them? Try especially to appraise your own knowledge and background in each area, *measured against the job sought*, and identify any areas in which you are weak. Be critical and realistic – do not flatter yourself.

4) Do some general reading in areas in which you feel you may be weak

For example, if the job involves supervision and your past experience has NOT, some general reading in supervisory methods and practices, particularly in the field of human relations, might be useful. Do NOT study agency procedures or detailed manuals. The oral board will be testing your understanding and capacity, not your memory.

5) Get a good night's sleep and watch your general health and mental attitude

You will want a clear head at the interview. Take care of a cold or any other minor ailment, and of course, no hangovers.

What should be done on the day of the interview?

Now comes the day of the interview itself. Give yourself plenty of time to get there. Plan to arrive somewhat ahead of the scheduled time, particularly if your appointment is in the fore part of the day. If a previous candidate fails to appear, the board might be ready for you a bit early. By early afternoon an oral board is almost invariably behind schedule if there are many candidates, and you may have to wait. Take along a book or magazine to read, or your application to review, but leave any extraneous material in the waiting room when you go in for your interview. In any event, relax and compose yourself.

The matter of dress is important. The board is forming impressions about you – from your experience, your manners, your attitude, and your appearance. Give your personal appearance careful attention. Dress your best, but not your flashiest. Choose conservative, appropriate clothing, and be sure it is immaculate. This is a business interview, and your appearance should indicate that you regard it as such. Besides, being well groomed and properly dressed will help boost your confidence.

Sooner or later, someone will call your name and escort you into the interview room. *This is it.* From here on you are on your own. It is too late for any more preparation. But remember, you asked for this opportunity to prove your fitness, and you are here because your request was granted.

What happens when you go in?

The usual sequence of events will be as follows: The clerk (who is often the board stenographer) will introduce you to the chairman of the oral board, who will introduce you to the other members of the board. Acknowledge the introductions before you sit down. Do not be surprised if you find a microphone facing you or a stenotypist sitting by. Oral interviews are usually recorded in the event of an appeal or other review.

Usually the chairman of the board will open the interview by reviewing the highlights of your education and work experience from your application – primarily for the benefit of the other members of the board, as well as to get the material into the record. Do not interrupt or comment unless there is an error or significant misinterpretation; if that is the case, do not hesitate. But do not quibble about insignificant matters. Also, he will usually ask you some question about your education, experience or your present job – partly to get you to start talking and to establish the interviewing "rapport." He may start the actual questioning, or turn it over to one of the other members. Frequently, each member undertakes the questioning on a particular area, one in which he is perhaps most competent, so you can expect each member to participate in the examination. Because time is limited, you may also expect some rather abrupt switches in the direction the questioning takes, so do not be upset by it. Normally, a board member will not pursue a single line of questioning unless he discovers a particular strength or weakness.

After each member has participated, the chairman will usually ask whether any member has any further questions, then will ask you if you have anything you wish to add. Unless you are expecting this question, it may floor you. Worse, it may start you off on an extended, extemporaneous speech. The board is not usually seeking more information. The question is principally to offer you a last opportunity to present further qualifications or to indicate that you have nothing to add. So, if you feel that a significant qualification or characteristic has been overlooked, it is proper to point it out in a sentence or so. Do not compliment the board on the thoroughness of their examination – they have been sketchy, and you know it. If you wish, merely say, "No thank you, I have nothing further to add." This is a point where you can "talk yourself out" of a good impression or fail to present an important bit of information. Remember, *you close the interview yourself.*

The chairman will then say, "That is all, Mr. _____, thank you." Do not be startled; the interview is over, and quicker than you think. Thank him, gather your belongings and take your leave. Save your sigh of relief for the other side of the door.

How to put your best foot forward

Throughout this entire process, you may feel that the board individually and collectively is trying to pierce your defenses, seek out your hidden weaknesses and embarrass and confuse you. Actually, this is not true. They are obliged to make an appraisal of your qualifications for the job you are seeking, and they want to see you in your best light. Remember, they must interview all candidates and a non-cooperative candidate may become a failure in spite of their best efforts to bring out his qualifications. Here are 15 suggestions that will help you:

1) Be natural – Keep your attitude confident, not cocky

If you are not confident that you can do the job, do not expect the board to be. Do not apologize for your weaknesses, try to bring out your strong points. The board is interested in a positive, not negative, presentation. Cockiness will antagonize any board member and make him wonder if you are covering up a weakness by a false show of strength.

2) Get comfortable, but don't lounge or sprawl

Sit erectly but not stiffly. A careless posture may lead the board to conclude that you are careless in other things, or at least that you are not impressed by the importance of the occasion. Either conclusion is natural, even if incorrect. Do not fuss with your clothing, a pencil or an ashtray. Your hands may occasionally be useful to emphasize a point; do not let them become a point of distraction.

3) Do not wisecrack or make small talk

This is a serious situation, and your attitude should show that you consider it as such. Further, the time of the board is limited – they do not want to waste it, and neither should you.

4) Do not exaggerate your experience or abilities
In the first place, from information in the application or other interviews and sources, the board may know more about you than you think. Secondly, you probably will not get away with it. An experienced board is rather adept at spotting such a situation, so do not take the chance.

5) If you know a board member, do not make a point of it, yet do not hide it
Certainly you are not fooling him, and probably not the other members of the board. Do not try to take advantage of your acquaintanceship – it will probably do you little good.

6) Do not dominate the interview
Let the board do that. They will give you the clues – do not assume that you have to do all the talking. Realize that the board has a number of questions to ask you, and do not try to take up all the interview time by showing off your extensive knowledge of the answer to the first one.

7) Be attentive
You only have 20 minutes or so, and you should keep your attention at its sharpest throughout. When a member is addressing a problem or question to you, give him your undivided attention. Address your reply principally to him, but do not exclude the other board members.

8) Do not interrupt
A board member may be stating a problem for you to analyze. He will ask you a question when the time comes. Let him state the problem, and wait for the question.

9) Make sure you understand the question
Do not try to answer until you are sure what the question is. If it is not clear, restate it in your own words or ask the board member to clarify it for you. However, do not haggle about minor elements.

10) Reply promptly but not hastily
A common entry on oral board rating sheets is "candidate responded readily," or "candidate hesitated in replies." Respond as promptly and quickly as you can, but do not jump to a hasty, ill-considered answer.

11) Do not be peremptory in your answers
A brief answer is proper – but do not fire your answer back. That is a losing game from your point of view. The board member can probably ask questions much faster than you can answer them.

12) Do not try to create the answer you think the board member wants
He is interested in what kind of mind you have and how it works – not in playing games. Furthermore, he can usually spot this practice and will actually grade you down on it.

13) Do not switch sides in your reply merely to agree with a board member
Frequently, a member will take a contrary position merely to draw you out and to see if you are willing and able to defend your point of view. Do not start a debate, yet do not surrender a good position. If a position is worth taking, it is worth defending.

14) Do not be afraid to admit an error in judgment if you are shown to be wrong

The board knows that you are forced to reply without any opportunity for careful consideration. Your answer may be demonstrably wrong. If so, admit it and get on with the interview.

15) Do not dwell at length on your present job

The opening question may relate to your present assignment. Answer the question but do not go into an extended discussion. You are being examined for a *new* job, not your present one. As a matter of fact, try to phrase ALL your answers in terms of the job for which you are being examined.

Basis of Rating

Probably you will forget most of these "do's" and "don'ts" when you walk into the oral interview room. Even remembering them all will not ensure you a passing grade. Perhaps you did not have the qualifications in the first place. But remembering them will help you to put your best foot forward, without treading on the toes of the board members.

Rumor and popular opinion to the contrary notwithstanding, an oral board wants you to make the best appearance possible. They know you are under pressure – but they also want to see how you respond to it as a guide to what your reaction would be under the pressures of the job you seek. They will be influenced by the degree of poise you display, the personal traits you show and the manner in which you respond.

ABOUT THIS BOOK

This book contains tests divided into Examination Sections. Go through each test, answering every question in the margin. We have also attached a sample answer sheet at the back of the book that can be removed and used. At the end of each test look at the answer key and check your answers. On the ones you got wrong, look at the right answer choice and learn. Do not fill in the answers first. Do not memorize the questions and answers, but understand the answer and principles involved. On your test, the questions will likely be different from the samples. Questions are changed and new ones added. If you understand these past questions you should have success with any changes that arise. Tests may consist of several types of questions. We have additional books on each subject should more study be advisable or necessary for you. Finally, the more you study, the better prepared you will be. This book is intended to be the last thing you study before you walk into the examination room. Prior study of relevant texts is also recommended. NLC publishes some of these in our Fundamental Series. Knowledge and good sense are important factors in passing your exam. Good luck also helps. So now study this Passbook, absorb the material contained within and take that knowledge into the examination. Then do your best to pass that exam.

EXAMINATION SECTION

EXAMINATION SECTION
TEST 1

DIRECTIONS: Each question or incomplete statement is followed by several suggested answers or completions. Select the one that BEST answers the question or completes the statement. *PRINT THE LETTER OF THE CORRECT ANSWER IN THE SPACE AT THE RIGHT.*

1. Claims for losses presented to insurers under policies covering property are USUALLY 1.____

    A. first-party claims
    B. presented under a bailee policy
    C. third-party claims
    D. presented under a trust-and-commissions clause

2. A person or organization holding the value of another in a position of trust is known as a(n) 2.____

    A. bailee B. fiduciary C. executor D. agent

3. In insurance, the theft of a part of a carton or package is denoted as 3.____

    A. larceny B. burglary
    C. theft D. pilferage

4. If a person is suing the insured, or holds a judgment, and is seeking to satisfy the claim out of the proceeds of insurance, this person USUALLY serves the insured or a claim representative with a(n) 4.____

    A. estoppel B. demand for appraisal
    C. breach of warranty D. writ of attachment

5. Obsolescence in merchandise reveals itself in each of the following EXCEPT 5.____

    A. style changes
    B. discoloration due to sun exposure
    C. overbuying
    D. incomplete assortment

6. When a covered peril serves to set in motion an uncovered peril, or a series of uncovered perils, the insurer is 6.____

    A. not liable for any part of the loss if the covered peril caused no damage prior to the inception of the uncovered peril
    B. liable only for the damage caused by the covered peril if the covered peril caused a loss before the uncovered perils created additional losses
    C. liable only for that portion of the loss proportioned to one part of the total number of perils involved in the loss
    D. liable for the entire loss created by the combination of mixed perils

7. When two or more items of property ordinarily insured separately are insured under a single item or when property at two or more locations is so insured, the policy is termed 7.____

    A. floater B. blanket
    C. specific D. comprehensive

8. Value and loss are USUALLY

   A. established by appraisal
   B. matters of fact
   C. established by arbitration
   D. matters of opinion

9. Any insurance other than contributing insurance is termed _____ insurance.

   A. specific   B. co-   C. re-   D. under-

10. The _____ method is MOST commonly used for pricing a building loss estimate.

    A. original cost
    B. unit cost
    C. replacement cost less depreciation
    D. cost per square foot

11. Selling property for the account of the _____ is termed *account of the loss*.

    A. trustee   B. insured   C. consignee   D. insurer

12. Claims for losses presented to insurers under policies covering liability are USUALLY resolved by means of

    A. adjustment   B. settlement
    C. litigation   D. arbitration

13. Personal property FIRST becomes a potential subject of insurance when

    A. raw materials begin the process that will make them into finished products
    B. items are stored or transported
    C. items are being sold or used
    D. raw materials are removed from the earth

14. In handling an automobile physical damage loss, there are four ways in which part or all of the automobile may be sold as salvage.
    Which of the following is NOT one of these ways?

    A. Disposal pools   B. Salvage agent
    C. Contract salvage sale   D. Sale by sealed bid

15. Which of the following losses would be covered under the standard fire policy?

    A. Soot in a chimney ignites and the intense heat discolors the wallpaper on the bedroom wall through which the chimney passes.
    B. An expensive tropical plant is placed on the hearth near the fireplace and is wilted and destroyed by heat from the fire.
    C. Drapes made from synthetic fabric, hung too near a woodstove, melt and scorch from the excessive heat.
    D. The insured inadvertently drops an expensive necklace into a wastebasket, whose contents are later emptied into an incinerator.

16. The term *improvements and betterments* refers to

    A. updating existing policies in order to reflect changing economic conditions, uses of property, etc.
    B. additions or changes made by a lessee at his/her own expense, which improves a rented property
    C. any changes or improvements made during the execution of repairs, as part of a loss payment, which decrease the possibility of future loss
    D. lifestyle changes which decrease the probable insurable interest of a bearer of a life or health insurance policy

17. Which of the following steps in the procedure for adjusting a mercantile stock loss would occur LAST?

    A. Recovering lost stock
    B. Surveying and estimating the situation
    C. Separating damaged and undamaged stock and putting it in order
    D. Establishing insured interests

Questions 18-20.

DIRECTIONS: Questions 18 through 20 are to be answered on the basis of the information below.

A stock of suits in a men's clothing store suffers smoke damage from an exposure fire. The adjuster and insured agree that if the stock is marked down 25%, it can be sold. The retail value of the stock is $60,000; the cash value (insured's cost less depreciation) is $36,000. Prior to the loss, the insured operated at a 40% gross profit margin.

18. If the stock is insured at selling price, the property loss is

    A. $9,000   B. $14,400   C. $15,000   D. $24,000

19. If the stock is insured for actual cash value, the property loss is

    A. $9,000   B. $14,400   C. $15,000   D. $24,000

20. The insured's profit loss is

    A. $6,000   B. $9,000   C. $15,600   D. $36,000

21. The amount that a mortgagee may legally claim is USUALLY the lowest of three given amounts.
    Of the following, the _____ is NOT one of these three amounts.

    A. amount of loss or damage to the property
    B. amount of loss or damage to the property, minus a proportionate reduction for the debt remaining on the mortgage
    C. amount of the mortgage debt at the date of the loss
    D. limit of liability under a policy containing an average, coinsurance, or contribution clause

22. Of the following, _____ is NOT a term used in claims or loss statements to describe a fire's place of origin.

    A. extended
    B. off premises
    C. on premises
    D. communicated

23. The difference between personal property and fixtures is usually determined by all of the following factors EXCEPT

    A. adaptation
    B. leasehold
    C. incorporation
    D. intention

24. To provide that the full amount of insurance continues during and after a loss, _____ are sometimes added to policies.

    A. ex gratias
    B. exclusions
    C. liberalization clauses
    D. loss clauses

25. Under a contract of bailment, the relationship between bailor and bailee ends when the

    A. bailee delivers property into the possession of the bailor
    B. bailor delivers property into the possession of the bailee
    C. bailee sells the property
    D. bailee incurs a loss to the property

KEY (CORRECT ANSWERS)

1.	A		11.	B
2.	B		12.	B
3.	D		13.	D
4.	D		14.	B
5.	B		15.	A
6.	D		16.	B
7.	B		17.	C
8.	D		18.	C
9.	A		19.	A
10.	B		20.	A

21. B
22. B
23. B
24. D
25. A

TEST 2

DIRECTIONS: Each question or incomplete statement is followed by several suggested answers or completions. Select the one that BEST answers the question or completes the statement. *PRINT THE LETTER OF THE CORRECT ANSWER IN THE SPACE AT THE RIGHT.*

1. To obtain a quick approximation of the cost of replacing a building, which of the following methods or systems is usually MOST reliable? 1.____

    A. Original cost
    B. Cost per square foot
    C. Unit cost
    D. Cost per cubic foot

2. Any equitable or legal estate, any right that may be prejudicially affected, or any liability that may be brought into operation by a peril insured against, is defined as a(n) 2.____

    A. open liability
    B. insurable interest
    C. party
    D. encumbrance

3. A manufacturer's inventory consists of all of the following EXCEPT 3.____

    A. finished stock
    B. material purchased for conversion into finished stock
    C. goods purchased for use in the conversion of materials
    D. goods in process

4. The failure to use that degree of care which is considered to be a reasonable precaution under the given circumstances is known as 4.____

    A. omission
    B. negligence
    C. commission
    D. malfeasance

5. A contractual provision to give up, abandon or discharge a claim, or an enforceable right against another firm or corporation, is known as a(n) 5.____

    A. release
    B. exclusion
    C. liberalization
    D. subrogation

6. To provide that the insurance shall not attach until the loss to the property surpasses a certain amount, or surpasses the amount collectible from other insurance covering the same property, _____ clauses are sometimes added to policies. 6.____

    A. deductible
    B. franchise
    C. liberalization clauses
    D. excess

7. Which of the following is NOT an operative definition of *proximate cause*? 7.____

    A. The dominating cause of loss or damage
    B. An unbroken chain of cause and effect between the occurrence of an insured peril and damage to property
    C. A cause which arises as a result of property damage
    D. The cause which directly produces the loss

8. In adjusting a business interruption loss, an adjuster estimates the business interruption value and the amount of loss, and tries to agree with the insured upon claim components.
   This adjustment method is termed the _____ method.

   A. forecast B. book statement
   C. workout D. line-audit

9. Fast-track claim handling procedures are USUALLY associated with _____ policies.

   A. automobile B. inland marine
   C. residential D. business

10. According to superior risk forms insuring mercantile stocks, the value of a loss of records, manuscripts, or drawings would NOT exceed the value of the

    A. records blank
    B. cost incurred for actually transcribing or copying the records
    C. records blank plus the cost incurred for actually transcribing or copying them
    D. records blank plus the cost incurred for actually transcribing or copying them, plus the cost of any materials needed to transcribe or copy

11. The calculation of a policy reserve is termed

    A. acknowledgement B. reckoning
    C. valuation D. processing

12. In natters of insurance, compensation or reimbursement for loss is called

    A. subrogation B. allocation
    C. remuneration D. indemnity

13. Which of the following building materials tends to sustain the LEAST amount of damage when submerged in flood waters for a short period of time?

    A. Wood products
    B. Gypsum drywall
    C. Plaster and lath
    D. Insulation and fiberboards

14. After payment of a loss, the assignment to an insurer by policy or law, after payment of a loss, of the rights of the insured to recover the amount of the loss from one legally liable for it, is termed

    A. delegation B. subrogation
    C. substitution D. designation

15. Provisions for limiting the use of salvage to sale as damaged articles are contained within the _____ clause of a property insurance policy.

    A. franchise B. excess
    C. brands and labels D. loss

16. Of the following, the _____ is NOT a type of payee usually encountered by an adjuster.

    A. person who has an equitable lien on the proceeds of the policy
    B. assignee of the claim

C. bailee of the property
D. garnishee or judgment creditor

17. The replacement cost coverage of most building policies provides that the cost of various structural parts of the building is to be disregarded in determining if the amount of insurance equals or exceeds _____% of the full replacement cost of the building.

    A. 20 B. 40 C. 60 D. 80

18. For a business interruption loss, what information does a Statement of Loss provide the insurer?

    A. Agreed period of suspension; loss of net income for period of suspension; addition to net income of cost of goods sold and non-continuing expenses for period of suspension
    B. Loss of net income for period of suspension; addition to net income of cost of goods sold; subtraction from net income of non-continuing expenses for period of suspension
    C. Agreed period of suspension; loss of net income for period of suspension; subtraction from net income of cost of goods sold and non-continuing expenses for period of suspension
    D. Loss of net income for period of suspension

19. Of the following, the _____ is an explosion, as defined with the intent or meaning of provisions USUALLY found in standard homeowners' or businessowners' policies.

    A. rupture or bursting of pressure relief devices
    B. rupture or bursting of rotating or moving parts of machinery, caused by centrifugal force or mechanical breakdown
    C. ignition of furnace *puff-back* gases
    D. electric arcing

20. The _____ policy provides protection for personal property, wherever the property may be.

    A. fleet B. extended C. floater D. blanket

21. Of the following, _____ is NOT one of the primary functions into which an insurer's claim representative can be divided.

    A. negotiating   B. evaluating
    C. retention   D. investigating

22. Each of the following is one of the three types of salvage usually assigned to a total automobile loss EXCEPT _____ value.

    A. rebuilding   B. junk
    C. parts   D. ground

23. If the peril *accidental discharge or overflow of water or steam* were added to a homeowner's policy, of the following, those caused _____ would be covered.

    A. by continuous or repeated leakage or seepage over a period of weeks
    B. to the system or appliance from which the water or steam escapes

C. by discharge or overflow coming from within plumbing, heating, or air-conditioning systems or domestic appliances
D. by or resulting from freezing

24. According to most standard fire policies, under which of the following conditions would an insurer MOST likely be liable for a loss?

   A. As a result of explosion that does not create an ensuing fire
   B. If hazard is increased by any means within the control or knowledge of the insured
   C. When the described building is vacant or unoccupied for a period of 30 days or less
   D. The insured's conversion of a dwelling to serve purposes other than those named in the original contract

25. Under the typical provisions of a standard homeowner's policy, assuming that each loss is caused by a vehicle not owned or operated by any occupant of the premises, which of the following *vehicle* losses would NOT be covered?

   A. Insured's clothing being torn when he or she is struck by a vehicle
   B. Clothing of insured's child being torn when he/she runs into a stationary vehicle in the driveway
   C. The insured's furniture being thrown from a vehicle as a result of an accident
   D. Insured's furniture, in or on vehicle, being struck by another vehicle

KEY (CORRECT ANSWERS)

1. D		11. C	
2. B		12. D	
3. C		13. C	
4. B		14. B	
5. A		15. C	
6. D		16. C	
7. C		17. D	
8. A		18. C	
9. C		19. C	
10. C		20. C	

21. C
22. D
23. C
24. C
25. B

TEST 3

DIRECTIONS: Each question or incomplete statement is followed by several suggested answers or completions. Select the one that BEST answers the question or completes the statement. *PRINT THE LETTER OF TEE CORRECT ANSWER IN THE SPACE AT THE RIGHT.*

1. In the estimation of a building loss, which of the following errors could be committed while preparing specifications? 1.____

    A. Overlooked items of repair or replacement
    B. Materials not priced correctly
    C. Duplication by subcontractors
    D. Inclusion of items that do not exist

2. Leasehold interest may be written to protect the interest of a lessee under any of the following conditions EXCEPT if the 2.____

    A. lessee is subletting the premises, or any part of them, at profit
    B. lessee is in possession under a lease that does not provide for cancellation or abatement of rent in case of fire
    C. rental value of the premises is less than the rent paid by the lessee
    D. lessee has installed improvements that have become the property of the owner

3. Which of the following is a type of multiple-line policy originally intended to provide both broad and all risk of physical loss coverage for businesses that mainly provide services, rather than for those engaged in manufacturing or merchandising? 3.____

    A. HPR
    B. MOP
    C. SMP
    D. Business owners program MLB-700 and 701

4. Of the following insured perils, _____ exists only on the broad form of personal theft policies. 4.____

    A. mysterious disappearance
    B. burglary
    C. pilferage
    D. robbery

5. An insurer's right of subrogation comes into being 5.____

    A. as soon as a loss is reported
    B. when the proof of loss is submitted
    C. when the claim is filed
    D. when the claim is paid

6. Typically, the actual cash value of a building is stated as the 6.____

    A. replacement cost
    B. replacement cost less economic depreciation
    C. replacement cost less physical depreciation
    D. market value

7. Of the following, an example of an expense incurred for the insured's benefit which is not incurred for the direct prevention of a loss under a policy would be the cost

   A. to repair a building damaged by a fire that began in the building next door
   B. of a watchman employed to prevent theft or accident after a fire
   C. of overtime paid to maintenance crew in order to hasten repair of a loss
   D. of replacing old open electric wiring with wiring in conduits required by municipal ordinance

8. What percentage of property losses are small claims that can USUALLY be solved by sending a repair bill to the insurer?

   A. 25   B. 40   C. 75   D. 90

Questions 9-10.

DIRECTIONS: Questions 9 and 10 are to be answered on the basis of the information below.

Ten farmers had each stored in the same elevator 1,000 bushels of wheat of the same grade. 2,500 bushels are damaged as a result of fire.

9. Which of the following is TRUE?

   A. The owner of the grain elevator should be liable to each farmer for 10% of the loss.
   B. The owner of the grain elevator will be liable to a single insurer, who will apportion the loss among the farmers.
   C. Each farmer would be called upon to bear 10% of the loss.
   D. Each farmer may make a differing claim by use of dated receipts.

10. Property like wheat mentioned above is described as _____ in legal language.

    A. fungible   B. substituted
    C. communal   D. apportioned

11. An insured reports a loss involving $125 in cash and $25 in personal property.
    The following clauses are TRUE under the homeowner's policy:
    - The insurer is never liable, under any circumstances, for more than the actual cash value, which in this case is $150.
    - The company is not liable for more than 115% of the excess over $50.
    - The maximum liability cannot total more than 100% of loss on unlimited items plus the amount of limitation on limited items.
    Based on the information given above, the payment to the insured will be

    A. $100   B. $111   C. $125   D. $150

12. Under normal conditions, which of the following tasks would be performed FIRST by an insurer's claim representative during the adjustment process?

    A. Examine pertinent records or documents such as deeds, bills of lading, etc.
    B. Examine the policy or policies
    C. Inspect the scene of the loss
    D. Meet the insured or insured's representative

13. In matters of insurance, the determination of a single sum which would be actuarially equivalent to an income stream is termed   13._____

    A. surrogation B. proxy
    C. transposition D. commutation

14. A preliminary investigation of a loss indicates that a painter, employed by the insured, set a building afire while burning off old paint with a blowtorch.   14._____
    Of the following, the insurer will USUALLY

    A. exercise its right to action against the painter
    B. reject the insurer's claim and refer the matter to the representative parties of the painter and the insured
    C. put the painter on notice and invite him to parti cipate in the loss adjustment
    D. pay the claim and present the painter with a bill

15. The amount of insurance a company has on a risk, including the amount it has reinsured, is called _____ line.   15._____

    A. flat B. net C. multiple D. gross

16. Prior to a loss, if the insured waives in writing any or all right of recovery against any party for loss occurring to the described property, the insurance will NOT be invalidated if a _____ clause has been included in the policy   16._____

    A. liberalization B. subrogation
    C. no control D. loss

17. If property improvements are repaired or replaced at the expense of the insured, a lessee, within a *reasonable* time after the loss, the insurer's liability shall be   17._____

    A. the actual cash value of the improvements
    B. a function of the unexpired term of the lease
    C. the replacement cost of the improvements less depreciation
    D. nullified

18. If the insured uses his own employees for repairs in the case of a business interruption loss, and premium is paid on overtime, how should the base and premium rates of labor be charged?   18._____

    A. Both the base and premium rates of labor should be chargeable to business interruption coverage.
    B. Both the base and premium rates of labor should be chargeable to the building or contents loss.
    C. The premium rate should be chargeable to the building or contents loss and the base rate to the business interruption policy if it reduces loss.
    D. The base rate should be chargeable to the building or contents loss and the premium part of the labor to the business interruption policy if it reduces loss.

19. The provisions for cancellation by the insured or the insurer vary in proportion to several factors.   19._____
    Of the following, the _____ is NOT one of these factors.

    A. effective date of cancellation
    B. the incidence or waiver or estoppel

C. basis for refunding the unearned premium
D. method by which notice is to be given

20. Which of the following losses is NOT covered under the NFIA definition of flood? 20.__

   A. The overflow of inland or tidal waters
   B. Rain, snow, sleet, hail and water spray
   C. The unusual or rapid accumulation or runoff of surface waters from any source
   D. Mudslides caused or precipitated by accumulation of water on or under the ground

21. In terms of an insurance contract, a building that is devoid of both furnishings and human habitation is described as 21.__

   A. unoccupied   B. vacant
   C. uninhabited   D. vacuous

22. The owner of a manufacturing plant takes out building insurance for his property, which contains two buildings. The coverage is $100,000 under a policy that contains a 100% average clause. The agreed sound value of all the buildings is $120,000.
   The insured suffers a loss to one of the buildings. The sound value at the location of the loss is $50,000. The agreed loss is total, $50,000.
   What will the payment be to the insured? 22.__

   A. $25,000   B. $41,666.67
   C. $50,000   D. $83,333.34

23. The amount of the insurer's liability under any business interruption policy containing a contribution clause will be determined by four factors.
   Of the following, _____ is NOT one of these factors. 23.__

   A. amount of loss sustained
   B. the businessowner's profit margin
   C. other insurance
   D. amount of any expense that has reduced the loss under the policy

24. Except when working under catastrophic conditions, an adjuster is NORMALLY expected to reach the scene of any loss within _____ hours after it is assigned. 24.__

   A. 6   B. 12   C. 24   D. 48

25. The purpose of an average or coinsurance clause may be nullified if 25.__

   A. it cannot be established that the loss was caused by a negligent third party
   B. value and loss are not measured on the same basis
   C. the policy does not contain a reduced-rate contribution clause
   D. any peril named in the claim is not named in the policy

KEY (CORRECT ANSWERS)

1. C
2. C
3. C
4. A
5. D

6. C
7. B
8. C
9. C
10. A

11. B
12. D
13. D
14. C
15. D

16. B
17. A
18. D
19. B
20. B

21. B
22. A
23. B
24. C
25. B

EXAMINATION SECTION
TEST 1

DIRECTIONS: Each question or incomplete statement is followed by several suggested answers or completions. Select the one that BEST answers the question or completes the statement. *PRINT THE LETTER OF THE CORRECT ANSWER IN THE SPACE AT THE RIGHT.*

1. Company cars are furnished to salespersons of a large organization. They use the cars for business purposes primarily. The car is kept garaged at the employee's home nights and weekends if not in use. The company services the cars and furnishes gasoline and oil. One employee also has a personal automobile which is covered by a family automobile policy. On a weekend pleasure trip with the family, the employee uses the company car, which is not prohibited, and runs into a tree, causing $1,000 damage to the car. Which of the following is TRUE? 1.____

    A. The employee is liable for all damage to the car, which is not covered under the family policy.
    B. If the employee's family policy is a comprehensive policy, the family policy insurer will pay the loss.
    C. Under most standard family automobile policies, the family policy insurer will accept liability for half of the loss.
    D. If the employee's family policy is a collision policy, the family policy insurer will pay the loss.

2. According to superior risk forms insuring mercantile stocks, the value of a loss of stock in process would be the 2.____

    A. replacement cost of stock plus labor expended, plus the proper proportion of overhead charges
    B. regular cash selling price, less all discounts and charges to which such stock would have been subject had no loss occurred
    C. exchange value
    D. replacement cost

3. A newly issued business paid for, plus reinstatements, minus lapses and cancellations is termed 3.____

    A. expansion   B. advance
    C. gain   D. net increase

4. Of the following, the adjustment method used MOST often on losses involving minor building repairs, or in replacing or repairing household objects, is the one where the adjuster 4.____

    A. and insured agree on the value of any personal property, after which the insurer pays and takes the property for sale as salvage
    B. and insured accept as a basis for determining the loss the record of cost of construction or purchase
    C. exercises the insurer's option to repair or replace the property
    D. and insured delegate the determination of loss to a single expert

5. Of the following, the _____ is NOT one of the three factors that must be established when adjusting most rent or rental-value losses.

   A. length of time that normally would be required to repair or rebuild the premises
   B. total amount of the rent, or the total rental value of the entire premises for the length of time on which coinsurance or average is based
   C. difference between the date the lease expires and the date the loss occurred
   D. weekly or monthly amount of rent paid

6. Each of the following is a commonly used method by which an insurer might undertake to give the insured written notice of cancellation required by most standard fire policy terms EXCEPT by

   A. certified mail addressed to the named insured
   B. ordinary letter sent first-class mail
   C. personal service of such written notice upon the insured
   D. ordinary letter sent by first-class mail, supported by an affidavit as to mailing and a post office receipt

7. In adjusting a mercantile stock loss in which the property has been completely destroyed, an adjuster by adjusting the insured's last inventory listings for all interim purchases and sales in units to the date of the loss.
   The method of adjustment being used is

   A. book statement   B. quantity analysis
   C. line-audit   D. periodic inventory

8. The specifications of a building loss estimate state each of the following in detail EXCEPT

   A. what work is to be done
   B. the labor force performing the work
   C. how work is to be performed
   D. what size, kind, and quality of material is to be used

9. Which of the following steps in the procedure for adjusting a business interruption loss would occur LAST?

   A. Approval of efforts to resume operations
   B. Fixing amount of business interruption value
   C. Audit
   D. Authorization of expense necessary to reduce loss

10. The practice whereby one party, in consideration of a premium paid to him, agrees to indemnify the other party, for part or all of the liability assumed by the latter party under a policy of insurance it has issued is called

    A. renewal   B. reinsurance
    C. retention   D. reimbursement

11. The loss to a building that is damaged beyond repair is determined on the basis of any combination of the following EXCEPT

    A. replacement cost
    B. conformity to valued-policy statute

C. market value
D. actual cash value

12. What is the term for an item of property that is personal in nature but has been so annexed to real property that it has become a part of the realty?

    A. Annex   B. Extension   C. Fixture   D. Tap

13. Most criticism of adjusters by the insured stems from apparent or actual

    A. fraud
    B. collusion
    C. nonconcurrency
    D. neglect

14. The type of coverage which insures merchandise, furniture, fixtures, and equipment against loss by burglary or robbery while premises are not open for business is

    A. open stock
    B. covered stock
    C. open cover
    D. protected stock

15. Rent, rental, and leasehold insurance may cover any of the following EXCEPT

    A. the value to lessees of the use or possession of the premises they hold under the lease
    B. the value to lessee of personal property used as appliances on the rented premises
    C. rents receivable from premises ordinarily rented but temporarily vacant
    D. rents actually received or paid

16. Which of the following is a classification of a fire in terms of its cause?

    A. Friendly
    B. Incendiary
    C. Extended
    D. Communicated

17. If a lease is cancelled, the lessee suffers a loss measured by the value of his or her interest.
    This value will be determined by each of the following EXCEPT the

    A. unexpired term of the lease
    B. returns expected in use of the premises, or subrentals to be collected
    C. length of time the premises are out of use
    D. rent to be paid by the lessee

18. Homeowners' policies often contain a provision of coverage for the replacement value of personal property by endorsement. The coverage under the endorsement is established as the smallest of four possible values.
    Which of the following is NOT one of these values?

    A. 400% of the actual cash value at the time of the loss
    B. The replacement value at the time of loss, less depreciation
    C. The cost of repair or restoration
    D. Special limits described in the policy

19. Under normal conditions, which of the following tasks would be performed LAST by an insured's adjuster during the adjustment process?

A. Apply limitation clauses and apportion the loss, if necessary
B. Try to agree upon value and loss with insurer's adjuster
C. Prepare inventory, estimate, or statement of value and loss
D. Give written notice of loss to each insurer

20. Of the following, in a Gross Earnings policy, it is TRUE that a Gross Earnings Form

    A. has a limitation by using a coinsurance clause
    B. is worded to pay for loss of profit, plus continuing expenses
    C. has a dollar limit of liability for each 30 days following loss
    D. is not worded to pay for net sales or other income

21. Which of the following would NOT be covered under the Dwelling Building and Contents Form of an NFIA policy?

    A. The home of Mr. and Mrs. Smith
    B. A grand piano stored in the basement of the Smith home
    C. A large barn used for milking cows and processing milk which will be sold to the local dairy
    D. The home of Mr. and Mrs. Hofstetter, which also houses Mrs. Hofstetter's parents and Mr. Hofstetter's parents

22. Of the following, _____ is a type of multiple-line policy that provides all risk property coverage for retail and wholesale mercantile risks, subject to the standard fire policy.

    A. commercial property floater
    B. MOP
    C. SMP
    D. business owners program MLB-700 and 701

23. In case of a loss of personal property in the hands of a merchant, each of the following values is a component of the loss EXCEPT

    A. invoice price   B. freight charges
    C. trade discount   D. receiving cost

24. Which of the following is NOT a detail included in an inventory?

    A. Specifications   B. Prices
    C. Quantities   D. Descriptions

25. The fundamental difference between waiver and estoppel is circumscribed by

    A. the insured's intent to abandon or surrender a right
    B. an act of neglect on the part of an adjuster
    C. the adjuster's authority
    D. any omission on the part of the insurer

KEY (CORRECT ANSWERS)

1. B
2. A
3. D
4. C
5. C

6. A
7. B
8. B
9. B
10. B

11. C
12. C
13. D
14. A
15. B

16. B
17. C
18. B
19. A
20. A

21. C
22. A
23. C
24. A
25. A

TEST 2

DIRECTIONS: Each question or incomplete statement is followed by several suggested answers or completions. Select the one that BEST answers the question or completes the statement. *PRINT THE LETTER OF THE CORRECT ANSWER IN THE SPACE AT THE RIGHT.*

Questions 1-2.

DIRECTIONS: Questions 1 and 2 are to be answered on the basis of the information given below.

An insured reports a loss of mercantile stock to the insurer, but the stock has been burned *out-of-sight.*

- Last physical inventory before loss, Jan. 1 $100,000
- Purchases, Jan. 1 to date of loss, April 4, including freight-in, and after deducting cash discounts $ 50,000
- Value of goods removed by sale to customers from Jan. 1 to Apr. 4:
  - Sales, at selling prices, after deducting returns, allowances, and discounts $ 75,000
  - Average markup realized on sales as established by previous history of the business $ 15,000

1. The value of goods that have been removed at cost is

    A. $10,000 B. $35,000 C. $60,000 D. $75,000

2. The value of the insured's stock on hand at the time of loss is

    A. $35,000 B. $60,000 C. $75,000 D. $90,000

3. None of the following types of losses would usually be covered in a comprehensive standard family automobile policy EXCEPT a loss due to

    A. freezing
    B. use of any automobile as a public or livery conveyance
    C. flood
    D. use of a non-owned automobile by the insured while employed in the automobile business

4. Cost indexes are TYPICALLY applied in the _____ method of building loss estimation.

    A. unit cost   B. original cost
    C. lump sum   D. cost per square foot

5. An item of property, insured for $10,000 under a policy that contains an 80% coinsurance clause, is damaged. Its agreed sound value is $15,000. The agreed loss is $10,000. The coinsurer contributes $2,000 of insurance.
What will the payment be?

A. $8,000   B. $8,333.34   C. $8,666.67   D. $9,600

6. In homeowners' and business owners' policies, a building is described but not classified according to each of the following EXCEPT

   A. covering of its roof
   B. number of stories
   C. purpose for which it is occupied
   D. construction of its walls .

7. In adjusting property losses involving a bailee, the time that the property was delivered to the bailee may be determined by all of the following EXCEPT

   A. bills of lading   B. invoices
   C. warehouse receipts   D. truck tickets

8. Generally, the burden of proving value and loss rests upon the

   A. insurer's claim representative
   B. insured
   C. insurer
   D. insured's adjuster

9. Each of the following is a typical source for the approximation of the actual cash value of a total automobile loss EXCEPT

   A. blue books   B. dealer quotations
   C. sticker prices   D. newspaper ads

10. When a bailee puts property in the possession of the bailor, and it is removed from the vehicle or premises of the bailee, the delivery is said to be

    A. approximate   B. actual
    C. constructive   D. virtual

11. Which of the following is an example of *cool* smoke damage?

    A. Tar stains on tile surface
    B. Soot deposit on ceiling
    C. Resin deposit on wood siding
    D. Penetration of glazed surfaces

12. When merchandise as well as records are destroyed in a businessowner's loss, there are several sources of information available to aid in developing a statement of the value on hand immediately before the loss occurred.
    Of the following, _____ would be LEAST useful in this respect.

    A. income tax returns
    B. duplicate purchase records from suppliers
    C. contracts of bailment
    D. bank statements of deposits and withdrawals

13. When damage necessitates the rebuilding or repairing of buildings or equipment involved in a business interruption loss, the loss period ends with the date on which, with the date of due diligence and dispatch, restoration could have been completed.
    Which of the following situations would NOT alter this condition?

A. Operating efficiency was restored prior to that date.
B. Employees of the insured failed to effectively expedite restoration.
C. Replacement of stock in process in manufacturing risks requires additional time.
D. The available supply of raw stock would have forced a shutdown at an earlier date.

14. Of the following, _____ is NOT one of the four fundamental methods that insureds and adjusters commonly use when approaching problems of value and loss with the expectation of reaching an agreement. 14.___

   A. survey and estimate
   B. assignment of arbitrator
   C. actual repair or replacement
   D. selling of salvage

Questions 15-17.

DIRECTIONS: Questions 15 through 17 are to be answered on the basis of the information given below regarding a business interruption loss.

OPERATING STATEMENT
Anne's Tailoring

Prior to Damage

Sales		$1,400.00
Expenses		
Materials	$500.00	
Labor	$500.00	
Rent	$250.00	
Other	$250.00	
Total Expenses		$1,500.00
LOSS		$ 100.00

SETTLEMENT CALCULATIONS
Anne's Tailoring
After Damage

Gain to insured as compared to prior to damage:
  Determined that material cost does not continue $500
  Determined that labor costs do not continue $500
  Total savings as compared to prior to damage $
  Loss to Insured $

Loss to insured as compared to prior to damage:

Sales $1,400

15. What is the total savings to the insured as compared to prior to damage? 15.____
    A. $1,000   B. $400   C. $500   D. $1,400

16. What is the total loss to the insured as a result of the damage? 16.____
    A. $1,000   B. $400   C. $500   D. $1,400

17. As a result of the damage, the insured is entitled to a payment of 17.____
    A. $400.00
    B. $1,500.00
    C. $2,900.00
    D. nothing, since the business was operating at a loss when the damage occurred

18. A legal claim to property or other value which may be protected by insurance is termed 18.____
    A. loss   B. interest
    C. dependent   D. encumbrance

19. Provisions for broadening or expanding coverage in accordance with changes in the company, without the incurrence of increased premium, are contained within the _____ clause of a property insurance policy. 19.____
    A. liberalization   B. subrogation
    C. mortgagee   D. loss

20. An insurance contract in which there is unequal bargaining strength between parties is known specifically as a(n) 20.____
    A. aleatory contract   B. unilateral contract
    C. personal contract   D. contract of adhesion

21. Which of the following steps in the procedure for adjusting a building loss would usually be performed LAST? 21.____
    A. Examining the property and surveying the situation
    B. Obtaining the appraisal
    C. Choosing a method of adjustment
    D. Establishing interests

22. When loss is determined from books and records, of the following the MOST desirable adjustment method would be adjuster and insured 22.____
    A. agreeing on the value of any personal property, after which the insurer pays and takes the property for sale as salvage
    B. accepting as a basis for determining the loss the record of cost of construction or purchase
    C. making or having made independent estimates, which they compare and discuss
    D. each selecting an expert and instructing the experts to examine the property or evidence bearing on it, in order to produce an agreed estimate

23. Which of the following steps should NOT be taken when determining the initial reserve to send to a company in the event of a business interruption loss? 23.____
    A. Estimate damage to physical property and pay a percentage to insured
    B. Estimate the period of suspension

C. Estimate approximate sales for previous year for those months calculated for period of suspension
D. Deduct cost of materials from sales for period of suspension and use that as a reserve

24. Of the following circumstances, NFIA coverage for seepage due to hydrostatic pressure would be provided when

    A. capped floor drains threaten to burst from the pressure
    B. sanitary sewers, filled near capacity, emit an unpleasant smell in drains, toilet bowls, and tubs
    C. pressure creates a dampness in concrete floors and walls that causes a room to feel cold
    D. pressure forces water through foundation walls, displacing slabs of concrete and flooding the basement

25. Most homeowners' policies covering the peril of removal establish an applicable limit, pro rata, for a period of _____ days at each proper place to which property shall necessarily be removed from or for repair of damage caused by perils insured against.

    A. 10　　　　　B. 30　　　　　C. 60　　　　　D. 90

KEY (CORRECT ANSWERS)

1. C　　　11. B
2. D　　　12. C
3. C　　　13. B
4. B　　　14. B
5. B　　　15. A

6. C　　　16. B
7. B　　　17. A
8. B　　　18. D
9. C　　　19. A
10. B　　20. D

21. B
22. D
23. A
24. D
25. B

TEST 3

DIRECTIONS: Each question or incomplete statement is followed by several suggested answers or completions. Select the one that BEST answers the question or completes the statement. *PRINT THE LETTER OF THE CORRECT ANSWER IN THE SPACE AT THE RIGHT.*

1. Of the following steps, it is NOT necessary to _____ after loss has been assigned under a business interruption claim.

    A. inform insured that business interruption losses are only covered if she can prove that business was operating at a profit before the loss occurred
    B. determine length of time necessary to restore physical properties and advise insured that coverage is limited to that length of time
    C. ask insured for access to specific income and expense figures
    D. explain the specific coverages and limitations of the policy to the insured

2. The replacement value of damaged property, without any deduction for depreciation, is the property's _____ cost.

    A. gross   B. replacement
    C. amortized   D. flat

3. Unlike most property insurance policies which limit the removal of debris to the debris of the property covered, the debris removal clause

    A. covers the removal of the debris from the peril insured against, limited to the debris of the property covered
    B. covers only the removal of the debris of the property covered
    C. covers the removal of all debris from the peril insured against, not limited to debris of the property covered
    D. does not differ from that found on most property insurance policies

4. Of the following types of damage, _____ would be covered by most standard fire policies.

    A. a countertop scorched by a hot cooking utensil
    B. a hole burned in a carpet by a cigarette
    C. a chair, placed too close to a burning hearth fire, receiving a blistered finish
    D. fabric or material scorched by a pressing iron

5. Which of the following types of losses would be covered under the standard collision coverage of an automobile policy?

    A. Damage due to freezing
    B. Glass broken during a theft
    C. Hitting a deer or other wild animal on a rural road
    D. Two-car crash occurring during use of a non-owned automobile by the insured

6. A schedule showing the limits of liability to be written by a ceding company for different classes of risks is termed

    A. superior risk form   B. loss form
    C. ceiling slip   D. line sheet

7. If several property policies are involved in covering an insured's property, a provision for the proportionate allotment of the liability among the policies would be provided by a _____ clause.

   A. pro rata, distribution
   B. apportionment
   C. proration
   D. subrogation

8. A business interruption policy provides coverage when the insured suffers a loss of

   A. revenue
   B. revenue that he would have earned during the time it takes to repair damaged property, and when insured can prove that the business was previously operating at a profit margin
   C. revenue that he would have earned during the time it takes to repair damaged property
   D. personal property due to natural disaster

9. A claim is made by an insured whose building policy contains a coinsurance clause.
   Amount of insurance $140,000
   Replacement cost $200,000
   Actual cash value $ 80,000
   Coinsurance percentage   80%
   Cost of repairs $ 10,000
   Depreciation $ 2,000
   Cash value of repairs $ 8,000

   On the basis of the information given above, the cash value collectible under the policy for the loss described in the figures, including the replacement cost endorsement, would be

   A. $6,400   B. $7,000   C. $8,000   D. $10,000

10. According to most value reporting clauses of business insurance reporting forms, the insured must report in writing to the insurer NOT more than _____ days after the last day of each calendar month.

    A. 2   B. 14   C. 30   D. 60

11. A Certificate of Satisfaction may exist as a separate document, or it may be incorporated, into the

    A. articles of subrogation and assignment
    B. proof of loss form
    C. non-waiver agreement
    D. property loss notice

12. In adjusting a business interruption loss, the amount of income lost _____ should be used to calculate a settlement for a period of suspension.

    A. and all expenses which the business incurred prior to the period of suspension
    B. as well as those expenses which are not necessary to continue during the suspension
    C. and the profit margin of the business prior to the suspension
    D. is the only information that

13. Mercantile stocks are covered under a businessowner's policy as business personal property, and are covered for

    A. dealer's selling price
    B. exchange value
    C. manufacturing cost
    D. replacement value

14. Which of the following is a type of multiple-line policy designed for large mercantile and manufacturing businesses with a high degree of fire protection usually in the form of sprinklers, fire-resistant construction, etc.?

    A. HPR
    B. Commercial property floater
    C. SMP
    D. Business owners program MLB-700 and 701

15. The purpose of a coinsurance or average clause is to

    A. allow the insurer to claim the median value, if any disagreement exists during adjusting, between the two irreconcilably different values
    B. assist the insurer in amortizing losses in cases of clear property depreciation
    C. apportion liability in the case of multiple policy coverage of a given loss
    D. provide for the reduction of an insurance payment in the case of partial loss of covered property

16. Which of the following is a difference between rent insurance and rental value insurance?

    A. Rent insurance is devised to indemnify an owner who is ousted from the premises by a loss.
    B. Rent insurance is devised to indemnify an owner for loss of rent.
    C. Rent insurance is extended to cover vacant premises.
    D. Rental value insurance is devised to relieve a lessee from paying rent for untenantable premises.

17. Of the following methods, _____ is MOST commonly used by insurers to give the insured written notice of cancellation.

    A. registered mail addressed to the named insured
    B. ordinary letter sent first-class mail
    C. personal service of such written notice upon the insured
    D. ordinary letter sent by first-class mail, supported by an affidavit as to mailing and a post office receipt

18. To find a rational formula for determining the proper amount of insurance to be carried on a building, insurers NORMALLY use _____ cost.

    A. replacement
    B. depreciation deducted replacement
    C. original
    D. market

19. In insurance, conditions which are natural to the insured premises are described as

    A. congenital
    B. intrinsic
    C. fundamental
    D. inherent

20. Nonconcurrent policies usually present questions related to each of the following EXCEPT

   A. exclusions
   B. value and loss
   C. limitations
   D. contribution and apportionment

21. What is a reinsurance facility for declaring and insuring risks of a specified category?

   A. Open cover
   B. Floater
   C. Contribution
   D. Direct cover

22. Provisions requiring the insured to carry insurance equal to a specified percentage of the value of the property covered are contained within the _____ clause of a property insurance policy.

   A. average
   B. apportionment
   C. pro rata distribution
   D. coinsurance

23. The difference between the ordinary payroll exclusion endorsement and the limited payroll exclusion endorsement, which may be added to the basic business interruption policy, is that in determining values and loss the _____ payroll exclusion endorsement deletes direct production

   A. ordinary; payroll after the first 90 days after the loss while the limited payroll exclusion endorsement deletes direct production payroll in the manufacturing form
   B. limited; in the manufacturing form
   C. ordinary; payroll while the limited payroll exclusion endorsement deletes direct production payroll in the manufacturing form after the first 90 days after the loss
   D. ordinary; payroll after the first 90 days after the loss

24. The replacement cost coverage of most building policies provides that there is no liability for the full replacement portion of the coverage (amount in excess of actual cash value) if the loss exceeds _____% of the insurance, unless actual repair or replacement is completed.

   A. 5   B. 10   C. 20   D. 35

25. Of the following, _____ is considered to be an item of personal property.

   A. a range owned by a landlord and installed for a tenant's use
   B. the electrical outlets of a rented structure
   C. a parking structure built by a tenant on the rented premises
   D. a refrigerator owned by a tenant

KEY (CORRECT ANSWERS)

1. A
2. B
3. C
4. B
5. D

6. D
7. A
8. C
9. B
10. C

11. B
12. B
13. D
14. A
15. D

16. B
17. A
18. B
19. D
20. B

21. A
22. D
23. C
24. A
25. D

EXAMINATION SECTION
TEST 1

DIRECTIONS: Each question or incomplete statement is followed by several suggested answers or completions. Select the one that BEST answers the question or completes the statement. *PRINT THE LETTER OF THE CORRECT ANSWER IN THE SPACE AT THE RIGHT.*

1. On small losses, the _____ report may be the only report submitted to the insurer. 1.____

   A. preliminary B. status
   C. interim D. closing

2. All of the following are losses or expenses not covered by a property policy EXCEPT 2.____

   A. excluded perils B. proximate loss
   C. consequential loss D. previous loss

3. Which of the following is NOT a procedure used to adjust total mercantile stock losses in the absence of perpetual inventory records? 3.____

   A. Add quantities purchased or manufactured during the period to the unit breakdown of the last physical inventory
   B. Deduct the net quantities of each product sold or shipped, as revealed by shipping records or invoices
   C. Add insurer's written statement of mysterious disappearances, theft, or deterioration since the last physical inventory
   D. Segregate last physical inventory into units of each product

4. Under commercial policies, *premises* is NORMALLY defined as 4.____

   A. the extension of all real property, including the grounds outside the building, associated with the building and plot in which the insured is conducting business
   B. the interior of any building of which a part of any size is occupied by the insured in conducting business
   C. the interior of that portion of any building which is occupied by the insured in conducting its business
   D. any real property on which a claim for insurance can be justified for any reason

5. In adjusting a business interruption loss, an adjuster authorizes the insured to carry out reparations and make expenditures necessary to resolve the claim.
   This adjustment method is the _____ method. 5.____

   A. forecast B. quantity analysis
   C. workout D. authorization

6. All of the following reasons account for 60-80% of insureds' complaints in all lines of coverage EXCEPT 6.____

   A. denial of claim
   B. unsatisfactory settlement offer
   C. compulsive litigation
   D. delays in handling claims

7. Provisions for covering property in multiple locations under the same contract, so that the value in each is considered the value in all, are contained within the _____ clause of a property insurance policy.

   A. average
   B. apportionment
   C. distribution
   D. coinsurance

8. As part of a building loss estimate, overhead and profit would equal _____% of the cost of materials and labor required.

   A. 5   B. 10   C. 20   D. 35

9. An automotive policy that covers all risk of physical loss is termed

   A. collision
   B. floater
   C. comprehensive
   D. blanket

10. The insured is protected against forgery and alteration of securities by Form

    A. 4   B. DF-1   C. G-401   D. H-1

11. Of the following, it is TRUE that an earnings form

    A. has a limitation by means of a coinsurance clause
    B. is worded to pay for loss of net sales, plus other income, less non-continuing expenses
    C. is not worded to pay for loss of profit or continuing expenses
    D. is worded to pay for loss of profit, plus continuing expenses

12. Each of the following is one of the three conditions that must be met in any claim for property improvements EXCEPT

    A. changes must have been installed or acquired at the expense of the insured as a tenant
    B. an insurable interest
    C. changes must be affixed to and a permanent part of the realty, as opposed to personal property
    D. changes must have been acquired through the transfer of a lease

13. On the basis of the following information, the cost of a businessowner's merchandise sold would be
    Purchases $3,500.00
    Ending Inventory $2,000.00
    Beginning Inventory $3,500.00

    A. $7,000.00   B. $2,000.00   C. $5,000.00   D. $9,000.00

14. An insurance contract in which one party makes an express engagement or undertakes a performance, without receiving in return any express engagement or promise of performance by the other, is known specifically as a(n) _____ contract.

    A. aleatory
    B. unilateral
    C. conditional
    D. adhesion

15. The measure of actual cash value in personal property losses is USUALLY the

   A. replacement cost new, at the time of loss, less depreciation
   B. value of such property on the secondhand market
   C. replacement cost new, at the time of loss
   D. original cost

16. In insurance, the felonious taking of personal property that is in the possession of another, from their person and in their presence, under constraint of force or fear, is denoted as

   A. larceny   B. pilferage   C. robbery   D. theft

17. Under normal conditions, which of the following tasks would be performed LAST by an insurer's claim representative during the adjustment process?

   A. Examine pertinent records or documents such as deeds, bills of lading, etc.
   B. Examine the policy or policies
   C. Inspect the scene of the loss
   D. Check any claim for possible errors and omissions

18. Each of the following is a contract of bailment EXCEPT

   A. bill of lading   B. sales receipt
   C. storage receipt   D. warehouse receipt

19. There are usually three limits of liability for physical damage coverage under an automobile policy, the lowest of which is the maximum amount the policy will pay.
Which of the following is NOT one of these limits?

   A. Cost to repair or replace with material of like kind and quality
   B. Actual cash value
   C. Original cost
   D. Limit of liability stated in the declaration

20. For approximating the actual cash value of a total automobile loss, the _____ method involves depreciation formulas.

   A. original cost   B. comparative
   C. market   D. current-year

21. In matters of insurance, a fire that remains confined to an intended place is described as

   A. safe   B. friendly   C. secure   D. domestic

22. During a mercantile inventory after a total stock loss, descriptions of the stock are taken from

   A. purchase records
   B. written statements from the insured
   C. invoices
   D. annual audits or profit and loss statements

23. Most automobile coverages are written with the limit of liability being the

   A. original cost   B. actual cash value
   C. exchange value   D. guide book cost

24. An insured's friend and neighbor, burning trash in the yard, leaves the fire unattended for a brief period of time. The trash fire extends to dry grass and travels to the insured's house, setting fire to the front porch. The neighbor feels badly and is in tears. The insured tells the neighbor not to worry because the loss is insured, and further consoles the neighbor with a letter releasing the neighbor of any negligence or financial responsibility, in return for $100. The loss is estimated to be $1,000.
Of the following, it is TRUE that the insurer is

   A. liable for $900 of the damage, and does not have the right to approach the neighbor for recovery
   B. not liable for any portion of the damage
   C. liable for $900 of the damage and has the option to attempt recovery of $900 from the neighbor
   D. liable for the entire loss

25. Which of the following statements is TRUE when determining gross earnings value under the gross earnings form?
Annual *gross earnings* are determined by the sales or sales value of production plus other income, less _____ the loss.

   A. non-continuing expenses for the 6 months following
   B. cost of goods sold for the 12 months following
   C. cost of goods sold for the 6 months prior to
   D. non-continuing expenses for the 12 months prior to

KEY (CORRECT ANSWERS)

1. D	11. D
2. B	12. D
3. C	13. C
4. C	14. B
5. C	15. A
6. C	16. C
7. A	17. D
8. C	18. B
9. C	19. C
10. A	20. D

21. B
22. C
23. B
24. B
25. B

TEST 2

DIRECTIONS: Each question or incomplete statement is followed by several suggested answers or completions. Select the one that BEST answers the question or completes the statement. *PRINT THE LETTER OF THE CORRECT ANSWER IN THE SPACE AT THE RIGHT.*

1. In contrast to the term *malicious mischief*, the term *vandalism* is associated with 1.____

    A. willful destruction
    B. criminal behavior
    C. injury to the property of others
    D. works of art and things of beauty

2. In automobile insurance, when the labor incident to one repair operation decreases the amount of labor necessary to perform the second operation, it is described as 2.____

    A. overlap
    B. redundancy
    C. included operations
    D. distribution

3. Under normal conditions, which of the following tasks would be performed LAST by an insurer's claim representative during the adjustment process? 3.____

    A. Negotiate an agreement with insured regarding value and loss
    B. Have a proof of loss executed for each policy or contract if no question of liability has arisen
    C. Apply contract conditions and determine the sum for which any policy, binder, or contract is liable
    D. Examine pertinent records or documents

4. Of the following steps in the procedure for adjusting a business interruption loss, _____ would occur FIRST. 4.____

    A. approval of efforts to resume operations
    B. examination and listing of policies
    C. audit
    D. authorization of expense necessary to reduce loss

5. If an adjuster were to examine a constructive total loss, which of the following would MOST clearly reveal the pitch and height of the building's roof? 5.____

    A. Cut of ceiling joists
    B. Evidence of flashing on a still-standing chimney
    C. Remaining pieces of roof support
    D. Position of fallen roof structures

6. Which of the following is attached to the standard fire policy in order to provide all risk of physical loss coverage other than those in connection with mercantile or manufacturing risks for all offices EXCEPT a physician's or a dentist's office? 6.____

    A. Commercial property floater
    B. Office contents form
    C. SMP
    D. Business owners program MLB-700 and 701

7. In adjusting a business interruption loss, which of the following statements is TRUE? Extra expense incurred that reduces _____ subject to any co-insurance penalty.

   A. loss is not
   B. claim is
   C. loss is
   D. claim is not

8. In matters of insurance, the difference between a fixture and a trade fixture lies in

   A. the extent to which the fixture has been incorporated
   B. the degree of the insurer's liability for the fixture
   C. whether or not the fixture is to be sold as a part of real property
   D. the purpose of the fixture

9. If a peril is set into motion by certain types of causes, the resulting loss will be covered. Which of the following types of causes is LEAST likely to create a peril that will be covered?

   A. Efficient
   B. Direct
   C. Consequential
   D. Proximate

10. Each of the following is one of the three basic areas of information an adjuster should develop when subrogation against a wrongdoer seems a possibility EXCEPT whether

    A. by law or by contract the third party is liable, even if not negligent
    B. the third party intentionally damaged the property of the insured
    C. the third party is financially able to pay damages, or carries insurance that will do so
    D. loss or damage was due to the negligence of a third party

11. Of the following, _____ is NOT considered to be one of the major elements involved in the estimation of building losses.

    A. overhead
    B. labor
    C. fees
    D. specifications

12. In case of disagreement, an adjuster and the insured may submit their disagreements to appraisal, reference, or arbitration.
    This method of adjustment is used MOSTLY in connection with losses involving

    A. personal property
    B. leasehold
    C. buildings
    D. business-interruption

13. Which of the following would NOT qualify a claim representative to handle flood losses?

    A. At least two years property loss adjustment experience involving the adjustment of wind, or wind and water losses
    B. At least five years experience adjusting property losses and at least two years experience adjusting property losses caused by wind or wind and water damage
    C. At least five years experience adjusting property losses if representative does not have required experience with wind, or wind and water losses
    D. Capability to prepare own estimates and validate all contractor's estimates

14. The rate for fire insurance charged on a structure as opposed to that charged on its contents is the _____ rate.

    A. building
    B. confined
    C. specific
    D. bonded

15. Which of the following should be considered when determining a settlement for a business interruption policy?

    A. Whether the business was operating at a profit or loss before the loss occurred
    B. The period of time necessary to restore the physical property and the income that would have been present during that period
    C. The period of time necessary to restore insured to the same level of revenue she/he enjoyed before the loss
    D. The likelihood that the business will succeed in the future

16. The general term for a form bearing the language necessary to record a change in an insurance policy is

    A. annexation   B. endorsement
    C. writ of attachment   D. amendment

17. A person takes out a standard windstorm/hail damage policy on a building property, which excludes the peril of collapse. Later, a strong wind blows over the building, which had been about to collapse due to a 6-foot snow load on the roof.
    Which of the following is TRUE?

    A. The entire loss is covered under the peril of windstorm, as it caused the collapse.
    B. That portion of the loss minus a standard penalty, levied against the insurer for failing to minimize the danger of a loss, is covered.
    C. Only the damage that can be proven because the snow load contributed to the building's collapse.
    D. None of the loss is covered, because the snow load contributed to the building's collapse.

18. A brief preliminary memorandum containing the essentials of the contract which are to be set forth in a completed policy is termed

    A. agreement to insure   B. written binder
    C. squinter   D. loader

19. The summary, included in a final claim report to an insurer, contains several main headings.
    Of the following, _____ is NOT usually one of the main headings in the summary included in a final claim report to an insurer.

    A. loss   B. sound value
    C. claim   D. original cost

20. Processed food products in the hands of a processor are valued at

    A. selling price
    B. selling price, less unincurred costs of selling
    C. replacement cost
    D. replacement cost plus shipping charges

21. The insured, under a standard family automotive policy, runs into a tree alongside a country road. Damage is slight but the car cannot be driven. The insured leaves the car and hitches a ride home. The next day, he reports it to the insurer, who sends an adjuster to meet the insured at the scene. During the night the car has been stripped of tires, radio, battery, and other parts.
Of the following, it is TRUE that if the policy _____ coverage, _____ will be covered.

   A. carries collision; but is not comprehensive, only the loss caused by the collision with the tree
   B. carries comprehensive; all loss
   C. does not carry collision; none of the loss
   D. carries comprehensive; only the loss caused by the collision with the tree

22. The purpose of abandonment clauses in property policies is to

   A. avoid a possible constructive total loss for the insurer
   B. assess penalty against the insurer for a denial of the insured's claim
   C. provide for all risk of physical loss, except in consequential theft losses
   D. increase the insurer's opportunity to sell a property as salvage

23. Of the following types of insurance contracts, an executory contract, the performance of which depends upon certain named contingencies, is the _____ contract.

   A. aleatory   B. bilateral
   C. conditional   D. contract of adhesion

24. When an adjuster attempts to value a mercantile stock loss according to the book statement method, verification of the results shown resolves itself into proving the reliability of the principal known components.
Which of the following is NOT one of these components?

   A. Cost of purchases or production
   B. Opening and closing inventories
   C. Net profit percentage
   D. Sales

25. How does a combined business interruption and extra expense form affect a basic business interruption policy?

   A. Provides coverage to insured for loss caused by inability of supplier to provide goods or services because of loss at suppliers' premises
   B. Suspends application of the coinsurance clause
   C. Extends limit of liability beyond the date it would take to restore facilities
   D. Provides coverage for extra expense necessary to continue business in a manner similar to that prior to loss

KEY (CORRECT ANSWERS)

1. D
2. A
3. B
4. B
5. B

6. B
7. A
8. D
9. C
10. B

11. C
12. C
13. B
14. A
15. B

16. B
17. A
18. B
19. D
20. B

21. D
22. A
23. C
24. C
25. D

TEST 3

DIRECTIONS: Each question or incomplete statement is followed by several suggested answers or completions. Select the one that BEST answers the question or completes the statement. *PRINT THE LETTER OF THE CORRECT ANSWER IN THE SPACE AT THE RIGHT.*

1. The measure of actual cash value in personal property losses, when the personal property proves to be irreplaceable, is USUALLY the

    A. amount the item could be sold for, according to an agreed appraiser
    B. value of such property on the secondhand market
    C. replacement cost of a like item, new
    D. original cost

2. An adjuster takes an inventory in order to value a mercantile stock loss by referring to a continuous recording of items received and items sold.
The type of inventory method being used is

    A. unit   B. perpetual   C. specific   D. periodic

3. Any personal property in use that is not specifically identified as furniture, fixtures, supplies, and machinery is denoted as

    A. apparata   B. equipment
    C. appurtenance   D. personal effects

Questions 4-7.

DIRECTIONS: Questions 4 through 7 are to be answered on the basis of the information given below.

A manufacturer produces five articles. The estimated costs used in the inventory are:

Product	Costs
1	$3.50
2	6.19
3	3.81
4	4.50
5	9.10

Production for the year was 6,000, 4,000, 3,000, 20,000, and 11,000 units, respectively, for the five articles.

Reference to the records discloses the following total expenditures for the year's operations: $40,000 for raw materials, $60,000 for direct labor, and $90,000 for overhead.

4. What is the total inventory cost of product 2?

    A. $11,430   B. $21,000   C. $24,760   D. $90,000

5. What is the total inventory cost of product 1?

    A. $9,000   B. $11,430   C. $24,760   D. $100,100

6. The total actual cost of production for the manufacturer was

   A. $57,290   B. $90,000   C. $190,000   D. $247,290

7. According to the inventory, the total cost of production was

   A. $57,290   B. $100,100   C. $190,000   D. $247,290

8. According to superior risk forms insuring mercantile stocks, the value of a loss of raw stock not manufactured by the insured would be the

   A. replacement cost of stock plus labor expended, plus the proper proportion of overhead charges
   B. regular cash selling price, less all discounts and charges to which such stock would have been subject had no loss occurred
   C. exchange value
   D. replacement cost

9. In insurance, a customer or business visitor is denoted as a(n)

   A. invitee   B. fare   C. patron   D. caller

10. An automobile loss occurs during a two-car collision in which only the automobiles are damaged. One of the drivers is insured under a standard family automobile policy. The insurer will ALMOST certainly waive the deductible if

    A. the driver's policy carries comprehensive coverage
    B. the insurer also covers the driver/owner of the other car involved in the collision
    C. there are towing costs involved
    D. the policy provides for supplemental payments

11. In insurance, the breaking and entering into the premises of another with the intent to commit a felony, whether or not such felony is committed, is denoted as

    A. larceny   B. burglary   C. assault   D. robbery

12. No suit or action on a policy for the recovery of any claim shall USUALLY be sustainable in any court of law or equity unless the suit or action is commenced within _____ next after the inception of the loss.

    A. 30 days   B. 90 days
    C. 6 months   D. 12 months

13. The list of individual items covered under one policy is the

    A. retainer   B. preamble
    C. schedule   D. inventory

14. An item of property, insured for $10,000 under a policy that contains an 80% coinsurance clause, is damaged. Its agreed sound value is $12,000. The agreed loss is $8,000. The payment will be

    A. $6,400   B. $8,000
    C. $8,333.34   D. $9,600

15. The resort to using books and records for valuing a mercantile stock loss becomes MOST necessary when

    A. a loss involves an appreciable quantity of out-of-sight merchandise
    B. a fraudulent claim is suspected
    C. extremely large stocks are involved
    D. some of the stock is stored off premises or in transit

16. What is the term for a portion of insurance transferred to a reinsurer?

    A. Coinsurance
    B. Redundancy
    C. Floater
    D. Cession

17. A mercantile inventory consists of

    A. goods in process
    B. finished stock
    C. stock purchased for sale
    D. material purchased for conversion into finished stock

18. In insurance, the term used for an extended reporting period longer than sixty days, but not unlimited, is

    A. protracted
    B. deferred
    C. midi-tail
    D. disclosed

19. An insurance payment is USUALLY not modified if the percentage of loss to value under a damaged, covered item of property is

    A. less than the percentage used in the coinsurance clause
    B. due to a peril that is not named in the policy
    C. equal to or greater than the percentage used in the coinsurance clause
    D. blocked by a subrogation clause

20. The owner of a manufacturing plant takes out building insurance for his property, which contains several buildings. The coverage is $100,000 under a policy that contains a pro rata distribution clause. The agreed sound value of all the buildings is $120,000. The insured suffers a loss to one of the buildings. The sound value at the location of the loss is $50,000. The agreed loss is total, $50,000.
    The payment to the insured will be

    A. $25,000
    B. $41,666.67
    C. $50,000
    D. $83,333.34

21. In adjusting property losses involving a bailee, the purpose for which the bailee holds the bailor's may be determined by all of the following EXCEPT

    A. bills of lading
    B. invoices
    C. warehouse receipts
    D. contracts to process

22. Claims for losses presented to insurers under policies covering liability are USUALLY

    A. first-party claims
    B. presented under a bailee policy
    C. third-party claims
    D. presented under a trust-and-commissions clause

23. If a loss is caused by the negligence of a person other than the owner of a property lost, destroyed, or damaged, the standard method of handling this loss is for the insurer to
    A. pay the loss to the insured with no subsequent action, due to the existence of a no control clause
    B. pay the loss to the insured, and then acquire a right of action against the person who caused the loss for the purpose of recovering the amount of the claim
    C. deny the claim of the insured and offer the services of a representative who will assist in recovering a claim from the negligent party
    D. deny the claim of the insured, leaving the matter to be negotiated between the insured and the negligent party

24. In casualty insurance, the annual cost per unit of the insurance company's exposure to loss is denoted as
    A. indemnity   B. risk   C. hazard   D. rate

25. When a retail businessowner reports the total loss of an article that has been sold on lay-away, the value and loss are USUALLY established as the
    A. replacement cost
    B. dealer's selling price
    C. replacement cost plus the proper proportion of overhead charges
    D. wholesale cost plus shipping charges

KEY (CORRECT ANSWERS)

1. A
2. B
3. B
4. C
5. B

6. C
7. D
8. D
9. A
10. B

11. B
12. D
13. C
14. B
15. A

16. D
17. C
18. C
19. C
20. B

21. B
22. C
23. B
24. D
25. B

EXAMINATION SECTION
TEST 1

DIRECTIONS: Each question or incomplete statement is followed by several suggested answers or completions. Select the one that BEST answers the question or completes the statement. *PRINT THE LETTER OF THE CORRECT ANSWER IN THE SPACE AT THE RIGHT.*

1. When a carrier bailee notifies the consignee that a shipment has arrived at destination, a(n) _____ delivery is said to occur when the free time expires before the consignee removes the goods.

    A. approximate B. actual
    C. constructive D. virtual

    1._____

2. Which of the following is a type of multiple-line policy providing broad property coverage for libraries, hospitals, and government buildings?

    A. MOP B. PIP C. SMP D. HRP

    2._____

3. Of the following, _____ is considered to be a fixture.

    A. a deck built by a tenant on the rented premises
    B. the electrical outlets of a rented structure
    C. items of furniture owned by a tenant
    D. a refrigerator owned by a landlord and installed for a tenant's use

    3._____

4. In insurance, a condition which may create or increase the probability of a loss is denoted as a(n)

    A. hazard B. peril
    C. endangerment D. risk

    4._____

Questions 5-10.

DIRECTIONS: Questions 5 through 10 are to be answered on the basis of the information regarding a business interruption loss given on the next page.

2 (#1)

OLIVIA'S GOURMET OLIVES
Statement of Loss
Earnings From Coverage

			LOSS	CLAIM

Period of suspension is
from 6/1/07-7/31/07

Loss and claim as determined:
Anticipated sales lost 6/1/07
   thru 6/30/07 $5,500

Less non-continuing expenses:
Cost of goods sold $1,500
Utilities   300
Delivery Costs   450
Sales Commission   1,000
Total Non-continuing $3,250

Loss as determined for period
   6/1/07-6/30/07 $

Liability is limited to 30% of
   $10,000 for each 30 day period
   after loss. Claim for this
   period is $

Anticipated sales lost 7/1/07
   thru 7/31/07 $5,500

Less non-continuing expenses:
Cost of goods sold $1,500
Utilities   300
Delivery Costs   450
Total Non-continuing $2,250

Loss as determined for period
   7/1/07-7/31/07 $

Liability is limited to 30% of
   $10,000 for each 30 day period
   after loss. Claim for this
   period is $

TOTAL LOSS AND CLAIM $ $

5. What is the loss as determined for the period 6/1/07-6/30/07?

   A. $3,250   B. $2,250   C. $5,500   D. $7,750

6. If insured has a policy which limits liability to 30% of $10,000 for each 30-day period after loss, the amount of the claim determined for the period 6/1/07-6/30/07 is

   A. not affected by this limit
   B. increased to the limit of liability for the 30 day period, which is $3,000
   C. reduced to the limit of liability for the 30 day period, which is $3,000
   D. added to the limit of liability for the 30 day period

7. What is the loss as determined for the period 7/1/07-7/31/07?

   A. $3,250   B. $2,250   C. $5,500   D. $7,750

8. If insured has a policy which limits liability to 30% of $10,000 for each 30 day period after loss, the amount of the claim determined for the period 7/1/07-7/31/07 is

   A. not affected by this limit
   B. increased to the limit of liability for the 30 day period, which is $3,000
   C. reduced to the limit of liability for the 30 day period, which is $3,000
   D. added to the limit of liability for the 30 day period

9. Based on the information supplied, the total loss for the period 6/1/07 through 7/31/07 is

   A. $6,000   B. $5,500   C. $5,250   D. $4,500

10. Based on the information supplied, the total claim for the period 6/1/07 through 7/31/07 is

    A. $6,000   B. $5,500   C. $5,250   D. $4,500

11. Of the following, the adjustment method by which adjuster and insured _____ is USUALLY confined to losses on stocks of merchandise.

    A. make or have made independent estimates, which they compare and discuss
    B. delegate the determination of loss to a single expert
    C. accept as a basis for determining the loss the record of cost of construction or purchase
    D. agree on the value of any personal property, after which the insurer pays and takes the property for sale as salvage

12. An insured takes out a policy on several buildings, after which the insured increases the fire hazard in one of the buildings.
    If all of the buildings are then damaged by a single fire, what type of clause would have to be included in the original policy in order for the insured to collect for damage to the buildings in which the hazard was NOT increased?

    A. Breach of warranty   B. Subrogation
    C. Liberalization   D. No control

13. During the adjustment of a mercantile stock loss, overpricing of a salvage inventory will

    A. result in a fraudulent claim
    B. reduce the out-of-sight loss
    C. have been computed on the same price basis as the book value
    D. increase the probability of a claim audit

14. Checking a claim consists of verifying each of the following EXCEPT that the

    A. amount is in order for the item claimed
    B. property is covered
    C. peril claimed to have caused the damage is one either named or not excluded in the policy
    D. damage was due to negligence of either the insured or a third party

15. Of the following types of insurance contract, the _____ contract is a mutual agreement of which the effects, with respect to the advantages and losses, depend on an uncertain event.

    A. aleatory   B. bilateral
    C. conditional   D. adhesion

16. Which of the following is an all risks of physical loss form?

    A. HRP   B. DIC   C. MOP   D. SMP

17. Of the following errors, committed in the estimation of a building loss, _____ falls into the category of errors made in computing the cost of the work.

    A. including property improvements
    B. improper consideration given to class of workmanship
    C. inclusion of property which is not covered under the policy
    D. duplication by subcontractors

18. An item of property, insured for $4,000 under a policy that contains a three-fourths value clause, is damaged. Its agreed sound value is $5,000. The agreed loss is $4,550. What will the payment be?

    A. $3,000   B. $3,412.50   C. $3,750   D. $4,550

19. Of the following, _____ is NOT one of the three primary elements of an insurance policy that must be agreed upon before an insurance contract is said to exist.

    A. property and location to be covered
    B. the parties
    C. perils insured against
    D. amount of insurance

20. Cost of goods sold $ 140,000
    Inventory beginning of year $ 60,000
    Average monthly inventory $ 40,000
    On the basis of the information given above, the merchant's stock turnover is

    A. 1.4   B. 2.3   C. 2.8   D. 3.5

Questions 21-22.

DIRECTIONS: Questions 21 and 22 are to be answered on the basis of the information given below.

A bailee's policy covering a public warehouse contains a trust-and-commission clause making it cover the property, but does not restrict coverage to the bailee's interest in, or liability to care for, the property.

21. If the insurance limits the value of the property, what adjustment is the bailee entitled to? 21.____

    A. Actual cash value
    B. Replacement cost
    C. Original cost
    D. Declared value

22. If the bailee fails to make claim for the bailor's property, 22.____

    A. the bailor is entitled to adopt the bailee's insurance and make claim
    B. the bailee has breached the contract of bailment
    C. no further claim can be made for the loss
    D. the insurer may file a right of action against the bailee

Questions 23-25.

DIRECTIONS: Questions 23 through 25 are to be answered on the basis of the information contained in the chart given below. Assume that Jayne's Gems has total sales of $20,000.

	Jayne's Gems Normal Expenses (prior to loss)	Non-Continuing	Continuing
Cost of goods sold	$ 9,000		
Salaries	4,000		
Rent	700		
Utilities	300		
Advertising	500		
Insurance	750		
TOTAL	$15,250		

23. After a business interruption loss, the insurer determines the following expenses to be non-continuing: cost of goods sold, rent, and utilities. The insurer also determines that $1,000 of the salary expense will be non-continuing and $50 of the advertising expenses will be non-continuing. Based on this information, the total for non-continuing expenses is 23.____

    A. $5,450   B. $11,050   C. $2,700   D. $3,550

24. After a business interruption loss, the insurer determines the following expenses to be continuing: $3,000 of the salary expense, $450 of the advertising expense and the insurance expense.
Based on this information, the total for continuing expenses is 24.____

    A. $8,350   B. $1,800   C. $4,200   D. $11,050

25. Assuming that Jayne's Gems posted sales of $20,000, the business interruption claim will amount to 25.____

    A. $4,750   B. $11,050   C. $13,200   D. $8,950

KEY (CORRECT ANSWERS)

1.	C	11.	D
2.	B	12.	A
3.	D	13.	B
4.	A	14.	D
5.	A	15.	A
6.	A	16.	B
7.	B	17.	B
8.	C	18.	C
9.	B	19.	D
10.	C	20.	C

21.	D
22.	A
23.	B
24.	C
25.	D

TEST 2

DIRECTIONS: Each question or incomplete statement is followed by several suggested answers or completions. Select the one that BEST answers the question or completes the statement. *PRINT THE LETTER OF THE CORRECT ANSWER IN THE SPACE AT THE RIGHT.*

1. To relieve the insurer from exposure to types of losses which are considered undesirable, uninsurable, or are not contemplated in the rate structure, _____ are sometimes added to a policy.

   A. exclusions
   B. stop losses
   C. estoppels
   D. escape clauses

   1._____

2. If the insured intentionally causes or procures a fire named in a claim, this is denoted as

   A. inside incendiarism
   B. arson by proxy
   C. inside communication
   D. extension

   2._____

3. When merchandise as well as records are destroyed in a businessowner's loss, there are several sources of information available to aid in developing a statement of the value on hand immediately before the loss occurred.
   Which of the following would be LEAST useful in this respect?

   A. Comparison of insured's business with firms of like kind and size
   B. Duplicate sales records from regular customers or purchasers of large quantities
   C. Credit reports
   D. Annual audits or profit and loss statements from previous years

   3._____

4. Under normal conditions, which of the following tasks would be performed LAST by an insured's adjuster during the adjustment process?

   A. See that the insured complies with policy requirements as to the handling of property after the loss
   B. Suggest to the insured any rearrangement of insurance that will provide better coverage
   C. Prepare inventory, estimate, or statement of value and loss
   D. Arrange for appeals from and adverse position taken by the insurer's claim representative

   4._____

5. A simple boiler and machinery policy contains a minimum of three basic forms to make a complete contract.
   Of the following, _____ is NOT one of these forms.

   A. policy jacket
   B. engineering and inspection form
   C. definitions and special provisions endorsement
   D. declaration and schedule form

   5._____

6. The type of policy that provides that a stipulated amount will be paid in the event of a total loss, in the event that a replacement cost cannot be determined is

   A. fleet   B. variable   C. floater   D. valued

   6._____

7. If property improvements are not repaired or replaced at the expense of the insured, a lessee, within a *reasonable* time after the loss, the insurer's liability shall be

    A. the actual cash value of the improvements
    B. a function of the unexpired term of the lease
    C. the replacement cost of the improvements less depreciation
    D. nullified

8. Another term used to denote either a waiting period or a probationary period in the terms of an insurance policy is _____ period.

    A. elimination
    B. encumbrance
    C. initialization
    D. string

9. According to superior risk forms insuring mercantile stocks, the value of a loss of media for or programming records related to electronic data processing equipment, including the data thereon, would NOT include the cost of

    A. reproducing the data on the programming media from duplicates or originals
    B. gathering or assembling information or data for reproduction
    C. the programming records blank
    D. media hardware

10. In adjusting a business interruption loss, the time element used in the calculation of loss begins from date

    A. of policy inception
    B. of loss
    C. that loss is reported
    D. that insurer determines as reasonable and accurate

11. When investigating a claim against an all risk of physical loss policy, the PRIMARY objective of the insurer's claim representative is to

    A. seek limitations
    B. verify loss
    C. seek evidence of non-accidental cause
    D. seek exclusions

12. When a contract is repudiated for a cause, _____ has occurred.

    A. recission
    B. withholding
    C. cancellation
    D. forbearance

13. A person or organization to whom possession of the property of others has been entrusted is called a

    A. guardian   B. bailee   C. trustee   D. custodian

14. Most alterations and repairs clauses cover temporary structures built on site, and materials, equipment and supplies that are on or within _____ feet of the premises described in the policy.

    A. 10   B. 50   C. 100   D. 300

15. Of the following adjustment methods, when an insured business employs its own maintenance and repair force, it is BEST for the adjuster and insured to

    A. arrange for the repair or replacement of the property on a cost-plus basis under proper check, then agree upon betterment as a result of the repairs or replacement
    B. delegate the determination of loss to a single expert
    C. accept as a basis for determining the loss the record of cost of construction or purchase
    D. prepare or have prepared agreed specifications for repair or replacement and submit these to be bid upon

16. The MAIN purpose that an endorsement extending the period of liability serves when added to the basic business interruption policy is to

    A. extend the limit of liability indefinitely beyond the date that it would take to restore the facilities
    B. extend the limit of liability 30 to 60 days beyond the date that it would take to restore the facilities
    C. limit the period of liability to within one day of the date that it would take to restore the facilities
    D. limit the period of liability on behalf of the insured

17. Buildings are said to be *obsolescent* when they show evidence of severe physical wear and tear, generally in excess of _____% of their replacement cost.

    A. 30   B. 50   C. 70   D. 90

18. When goods are shipped free on board, the shipper is responsible only until the goods have been placed on board the vessel or freight car or truck or other means of transport. Thereafter, the _____ is responsible for the risk.

    A. bailee   B. assignee
    C. fiduciary   D. consignee

19. A subrogation clause is included in a policy for the specific release of a(n) _____ from liability for a loss.

    A. insured
    B. undesignated third party
    C. insurer
    D. tort-feasor

20. Which of the following losses would be covered under the general property form of an NFIA policy?

    A. Records kept in an office building identifying all profits, losses and contracts of the owner
    B. The swimming pool of a hotel
    C. Landscaping surrounding the damaged building
    D. Fire extinguishing equipment kept in an office building to be used in the event of a fire emergency

21. An employee of the insured has stored flammable materials in a negligent manner, causing a fire that damages the insured's building.
If the insured were to collect for the damage, it would be due to provisions supplied by the policy's _____ clause.

    A. liberalization
    B. electrical apparatus
    C. work and materials
    D. no control

22. The MOST practical approach for evaluating a total automobile loss is the _____ method.

    A. original cost
    B. comparative
    C. market
    D. current-year

23. The MOST significant factor in approximating a building loss estimate would USUALLY be

    A. labor
    B. overhead
    C. fees
    D. materials

24. What is the term used to describe an accident that involves two or more people?

    A. Extended
    B. Common
    C. Chancel
    D. Communicated

25. When adjusting a loss under the policy of a bailor covering personal property that has been lost or damaged while in the possession, in transit, of a common carrier, an adjuster should fix value and loss and have the insured furnish certain papers.
Of the following, _____ is NOT one of these documents.

    A. bill of lading
    B. contract to process
    C. invoice
    D. consignee's affidavit

KEY (CORRECT ANSWERS)

1. A	11. D
2. A	12. A
3. A	13. B
4. B	14. C
5. B	15. A
6. D	16. B
7. B	17. A
8. A	18. D
9. B	19. D
10. B	20. D

21. D
22. B
23. A
24. B
25. B

TEST 3

DIRECTIONS: Each question or incomplete statement is followed by several suggested answers or completions. Select the one that BEST answers the question or completes the statement. *PRINT THE LETTER OF THE CORRECT ANSWER IN THE SPACE AT THE RIGHT.*

1. In homeowners' and businessowners' policies, a building is classified PRIMARILY according to the

    A. covering of its roof
    B. number of stories
    C. purpose for which it is occupied
    D. construction of its walls

    1.____

2. An insurance contract that can be performed only by the person with whom the contract was made, and which therefore is not binding to the executor, is known specifically as a(n) _____ contract.

    A. aleatory   B. unilateral
    C. conditional   D. personal

    2.____

3. The purpose of a fire clause in a lease is to

    A. prevent the tenant from escaping liability for a fire that was caused due to his/her negligence
    B. protect the owner from loss of rent due to a fire loss
    C. apportion insurance for a fire loss between the tenant and the owner
    D. relieve the tenant from paying rent for premises rendered untenantable by a fire loss

    3.____

4. Which of the following steps in the procedure for adjusting a mercantile stock loss would occur FIRST?

    A. Checking the coverage
    B. Surveying and estimating the situation
    C. Separating damaged and undamaged stock and putting it in order
    D. Recovering lost stock

    4.____

5. Of the following methods, by which an insurer might undertake to give the insured written notice of cancellation, MOST likely to involve the question of preservation of evidence would be

    A. registered mail addressed to the named insured
    B. ordinary letter sent first-class mail
    C. personal service of such written notice upon the insured
    D. ordinary letter sent by first-class mail, supported by an affidavit as to mailing and a post office receipt

    5.____

6. An amount added to the basic rate or premium to cover expense to the insurance company in securing and maintaining a business is termed

    A. endorsement   B. loading
    C. stuffing   D. amendment

    6.____

7. Which of the following is a type of multiple-line policy specially designed for small- to medium-sized businesses?

    A. Business owners program MLB-700 and 701
    B. MOP
    C. SMP
    D. PIP

8. In order to qualify for an investigation by the National Automobile Theft Bureau, a member insurer's investigation into a fire loss should reveal at least one of three situations. Which of the following would NOT warrant an investigation?

    A. Evidence of serious mechanical failure of the automobile prior to the fire
    B. Evidence of extensive glass damage to the automobile prior to the fire
    C. Discrepancies in statements between the insured and witnesses
    D. Previous automobile loss suffered by the insured

9. Of the following, an example of consequential loss is the cost

    A. to repair a building damaged by a fire that began in the building next door
    B. of a watchman employed to prevent theft or accident after a fire
    C. of overtime paid to maintenance crew in order to hasten repair of a loss
    D. of replacing old open electric wiring with wiring in conduits required by municipal ordinance

10. Of the following situations, a bailee, other than a carrier, would be liable ONLY for the loss of a bailor's property due to the bailee's negligence if the bailee

    A. agreed to keep the property insured
    B. were liable for loss according to prevailing trade customs
    C. entered a standard contract of bailment
    D. assumed further liability for causes other than negligence

11. An insured reports a loss involving $150 in cash and $250 in personal property. The following clauses are true under the homeowner's policy:
    - There is a limit of $100 on money.
    - The insurer is never liable, under any circumstances, for more than the actual cash value, which in this case is $400.
    - On losses under $500, the company is not liable for more than 125% of the excess over $100.
    - When an item, such as money, is subject to a policy limitation, the maximum liability cannot total more than 100% of loss on unlimited items plus the amount of limitation on limited items.

    On the basis of the information given above, what will the payment be to the insured?

    A. $300   B. $325   C. $350   D. $375

12. In the absence of a lease requirement to replace improvements and betterments made by the lessee, the measure of the lessee's insurable interest is USUALLY

    A. the cost of improvements made by the lessee
    B. the cost of improvements made by the lessee, minus a proportionate reduction for the expected useful value of the property based on life expectancy of the lessee

C. the cost of improvements made by the lessee, minus a proportionate reduction for the expired time of the lease
D. a proportionate fraction based on the life expectancy of the lessee

13. Which of the following perils is USUALLY covered under both forms of an NFIA policy? 13.____

    A. Pro rata coverage for 30 days at locations to which property must be moved to protect it
    B. Peril of removal
    C. Loss resulting from neglect of insured to use reasonable means to save and preserve property at the time of the flood
    D. Loss resulting from neglect of insured to use reasonable means to save and preserve property after the flood

14. An insured building under a standard building and structure policy has been damaged. The building does not have a basement. 14.____
    Of the following costs, _____ would USUALLY NOT be covered.

    A. replacement of buckled floorboards
    B. excavation below ground surface
    C. drilling of wall/floor boundary ventilation holes
    D. cleaning plate glass

15. The PRIMARY purpose a statement of loss serves when determining the amount of the claim for a business interruption loss is to record all 15.____

    A. the details and figures the adjuster used to determine value, loss, and claim
    B. assets, liabilities, and resultant net worth of insured at the time of loss
    C. revenue and expenses of insured for a specific period of time
    D. revenue, expenses, assets, liabilities, and resultant net worth immediately after the loss occurred

16. A person takes out a standard fire policy which does not cover the peril of explosion. Some time later, an explosion occurs, followed by a fire which causes damage to parts of the insured's property. 16.____
    Which of the following is TRUE?

    A. Only the damage caused by the explosion is covered, since the explosion occurred first.
    B. Only the damage caused by the fire is covered.
    C. None of the damage is covered, since the explosion occurred first.
    D. All of the damage to the insured's property is covered.

17. Which of the following statements is a definition of gross earnings as defined on a business interruption policy? 17.____

    A. Sales less cost of material sold and all other expenses which are not shown on the profit and loss statement as overhead
    B. Sales, plus other income, less all expenses which are not necessary to continue after loss
    C. Sales plus cost of material sold and sales, less other income
    D. Gross earnings as defined on the policy is sales, plus other income, less cost of goods sold

18. An insured, driving on a back road on a dark night, collides with a cow, causing damage to the car. The policy is a standard family automobile policy.
    Of the following, it is TRUE that

    A. if the policy contains collision coverage, the damage is not covered
    B. the damage is covered under the comprehensive portion of the policy
    C. if the policy contains comprehensive coverage, the insurer is not liable for towing costs
    D. the damage is covered under the collision portion of the policy

19. Under normal conditions, which of the following tasks would be performed FIRST by an insurer's claim representative during the adjustment process?

    A. Choose the method of adjustment to be used
    B. Check any claim for possible errors and omissions
    C. Estimate the situation and the probable results of adjustments made according to different methods that might be used to determine value and loss
    D. Have proof of loss executed if no question of liability exists

20. In order to reserve subrogation rights for a specific claim, an insurer's representative will typically obtain all of the following EXCEPT

    A. subrogation agreement   B. release form
    C. loan receipt   D. trust agreement

21. In insurance, the fraudulent taking of personal property that belongs to another without that person's consent, with the intent to deprive the owner of its value, is denoted as

    A. larceny   B. burglary   C. robbery   D. pilferage

22. The assignment to an insurer by terms of the policy or by law, after payment of a loss, of the rights of the insured to recover the amount of the loss from one legally liable for it, is known as

    A. malingering   B. liability
    C. encumbrance   D. subrogation

23. According to superior risk forms insuring mercantile stocks, the value of a loss of finished stock manufactured by the insured would be the

    A. replacement cost of stock plus labor expended, plus the proper proportion of overhead charges
    B. regular cash selling price, less all discounts and charges to which such stock would have been subject had no loss occurred
    C. exchange value
    D. replacement cost

24. An insurer's subrogation rights can arise from

    A. damage done to the insured's property by the wrongful act of another
    B. a contractual relation between the insured and a person who is charged with responsibility for the insured's property
    C. A above *only*
    D. A and B above

25. An adjuster takes an inventory in order to value a mercantile stock loss by physically counting each item of stock.
    What type of inventory method is being used?

    A. Unit   B. Perpetual   C. Specific   D. Periodic

KEY (CORRECT ANSWERS)

1. C
2. D
3. D
4. A
5. C

6. B
7. A
8. B
9. D
10. C

11. C
12. C
13. A
14. B
15. A

16. B
17. D
18. B
19. C
20. B

21. A
22. D
23. B
24. D
25. D

EXAMINATION SECTION
TEST 1

DIRECTIONS: Each question or incomplete statement is followed by several suggested answers or completions. Select the one that BEST answers the question or completes the statement. *PRINT THE LETTER OF THE CORRECT ANSWER IN THE SPACE AT THE RIGHT.*

1. Each of the following is one of the four upper limits for which the insurer is liable under the standard fire policy EXCEPT the

    A. cost to repair or replace with material of like kind and quality
    B. interest of the insured
    C. projected future cash value
    D. amount of insurance

    1.____

2. In boiler and machinery policies, a sudden and accidental breakdown of the insured object, or a part thereof, which manifests itself at the time of its occurrence by physical damage to the object that necessitates repair or replacement, is specifically denoted as a(n)

    A. accident   B. incident
    C. occasion   D. occurrence

    2.____

3. Which of the following losses would NOT be covered by an all risk of physical loss policy?

    A. Water damage to furniture caused by a sudden rupture in plumbing
    B. The discoloration of kitchen wallpaper above the stove, caused by repeated smoke/grease exposure from the stove and oven
    C. Roof shingles split by hailstones
    D. Water damage to the interior of the house, caused by a sprinkler inadvertently turned on by a child of the insured

    3.____

4. Of the following, _____ is NOT a type of reporting form.

    A. open cover   B. stock reporting
    C. general cover   D. multiple-location

    4.____

5. If leased premises are damaged by a fire that prevents the lessee from using them or from collecting subrentals, but the lease remains in force, the loss suffered by the lessee will be determined by each of the following EXCEPT the

    A. unexpired term of the lease
    B. returns expected in use of the premises, or subrentals to be collected
    C. length of time the premises are out of use
    D. terms of any subleases providing for the abatement or continuance of rent

    5.____

6. The adjustment of policy benefits due to a change of exposure, or the existence of other insurance is termed

    A. allocation   B. distribution
    C. apportionment   D. proration

    6.____

7. In adjusting a mercantile stock loss in which the property has been completely destroyed, an adjuster makes an approximate computation of the stock value, in total, from the financial accounts of inventories, sales, and purchases.
What method of adjustment is being used?

   A. Book statement
   B. Quantity analysis
   C. Line-audit
   D. Unit

8. If property improvements are repaired or replaced at the expense of others for the use of the insured, a lessee, the insurer's liability shall be

   A. the actual cash value of the improvements
   B. a function of the unexpired term of the lease
   C. the replacement cost of the improvements less depreciation
   D. nullified

9. What is another term for a deductible?

   A. Waiver
   B. Limit of liability
   C. Loss retention
   D. Estoppel

10. Under a contract of bailment, the relationship between bailor and bailee begins when the

    A. bailee delivers property into the possession of the bailor
    B. bailor delivers property into the possession of the bailee
    C. bailee sells the property
    D. raw stock of the property is in the possession of the bailee

11. Of the following, the adjustment method in which adjuster and insured _____ is used LEAST often.

    A. agree on the value of any personal property, after which the insurer pays and takes the property for sale as salvage
    B. go over property together and try to reach an agreement
    C. make or have made independent estimates, which they compare and discuss
    D. delegate the determination of amount of loss to a single expert

12. In adjusting most rent or rental-value losses, the length of time normally required to restore the premises can be determined by one of three commonly used methods.
Which of the following is NOT one of the three?

    A. Repairing by allowing the actual repairs to be made and accounting for the time
    B. A cost-per-square-foot approximation
    C. Appraisal
    D. Estimation with or without the help of a builder

13. Physical depreciation of personal property is USUALLY based on

    A. life expectancy
    B. environmental factors
    C. the purpose for which items are used
    D. current resale value

14. According to most value reporting clauses of business insurance reporting forms, the insured must report each of the following in writing in order to maintain full coverage EXCEPT

   A. exact location of all property covered
   B. specific insurance in force at each location on the last day of each calendar month
   C. any contracts of bailment that have been agreed upon since the last report
   D. total cash value of property at each location

14.____

Questions 15-16.

DIRECTIONS: Questions 15 and 16 are to be answered on the basis of the information given below about the insured (Dog Groomers, Inc.) after their insurance settlement following a fire.

```
Income from insurance company                $1,000.00
Continuing Expenses
  Rent              $500.00
  Other expenses    $700.00
```

15. The total expenses for the insured are

   A. $2,200.00   B. $1,000.00   C. $1,500.00   D. $1,200.00

15.____

16. The position of the insured after the settlement is a

   A. profit of $1,200.00   B. profit of $200.00
   C. loss of $200.00   D. loss of $1,200.00

16.____

17. How does a contingent business interruption endorsement affect a basic business interruption policy?

   A. Suspends application of the co-insurance clause
   B. Extends limit of liability beyond the date it would take to restore facilities
   C. Provides coverage to insured for loss caused by inability of supplier to provide goods or services because of loss at suppliers' premises
   D. Provides coverage for extra expense necessary to continue business in a manner similar to that prior to loss

17.____

18. Of the following, the FIRST task performed by an insured's adjuster during the adjustment process under normal conditions would be to

   A. make arrangement for appraisal in case of disagreement as to value and loss
   B. give written notice of loss to each insurer
   C. try to agree upon value and loss with insurer's adjuster
   D. facilitate the inspection of property by insurer's adjuster

18.____

19. Which of the following steps in the procedure for adjusting a building loss would usually be performed FIRST?

   A. Establishing interests
   B. Getting the insured's story
   C. Choosing a method of adjustment
   D. Examining the property and surveying the situation

19.____

20. If the insured does not keep a profit and loss statement for his business, which of the following sources would provide the MOST comprehensive information in the adjustment of a business interruption loss?

    A. Federal income tax return
    B. Balance sheet
    C. Receipts from the business
    D. Salary records

21. Under MOST policies, there is no insurer liability for loss due to vandalism or malicious mischief if the insured's buildings have been vacant for a period of _____ consecutive days immediately preceding the loss.

    A. 10   B. 30   C. 60   D. 90

22. Of the following, the _____ report raises questions of expediency or liability to insurers.

    A. preliminary   B. status
    C. interim   D. closing

23. Physical depreciation in merchandise reveals itself in each of the following EXCEPT

    A. irregular sizes
    B. fermentation of dried food products
    C. discoloration due to sun exposure
    D. flyspecks

24. A legal doctrine which may be used to prevent a person or organization from denying legal responsibility is termed

    A. ex gratia   B. obligor   C. binder   D. estoppel

25. Of the following, the adjustment method in which adjuster and insured _____ is MOST often used on large or complex machinery and fixture losses.

    A. prepare or have prepared agreed specifications for repair or replacement and submit these to be bid upon
    B. each select an expert and instruct the experts to examine the property or evidence bearing on it, in order to produce an agreed estimate
    C. agree on the value of any personal property, after which the insurer pays and takes the property for sale as salvage
    D. arrange for the repair or replacement of the property on a cost-plus basis under proper check, then agree upon betterment as a result of the repairs or replacement

KEY (CORRECT ANSWERS)

1.	C	11.	D
2.	A	12.	B
3.	B	13.	A
4.	A	14.	C
5.	A	15.	D
6.	D	16.	C
7.	A	17.	C
8.	D	18.	B
9.	C	19.	B
10.	B	20.	A

21. B
22. C
23. A
24. D
25. A

TEST 2

DIRECTIONS: Each question or incomplete statement is followed by several suggested answers or completions. Select the one that BEST answers the question or completes the statement. *PRINT THE LETTER OF THE CORRECT ANSWER IN THE SPACE AT THE RIGHT.*

1. Which of the following errors, committed in the estimation of a building loss, falls into the category of errors made in taking field notes?

    A. Including property improvements
    B. Improper consideration given to class of workmanship
    C. Inclusion Of property which is not covered under the policy
    D. Duplication by subcontractors

    1.___

2. In the event of a business interruption loss, _____ annual profit and loss statements would be sufficient to determine gross earnings value and loss sustained.

    A. at least 1   B. at least 3
    C. at least 10   D. no

    2.___

3. Two women each put up $60,000 to buy a building on speculation. Each has an undivided half interest in the property. One of the owners takes out a policy of insurance covering fire and extended coverage for $100,000, the value of the building, in her name only. Shortly thereafter, a fire causes damage of $80,000.
The insurer's liability to the policy holder is

    A. $20,000   B. $40,000   C. $60,000   D. $80,000

    3.___

4. The assumption of risk of loss through the use of non-insurance, self-insurance, or deductibles is termed

    A. recission   B. conjecture
    C. retention   D. underinsurance

    4.___

5. Of the following losses, _____ would be covered according to a simple boiler and machinery policy.

    A. leakage at any valve or fitting
    B. internal explosion that does not occur within a furnace structure
    C. the functioning of any safety or protective device
    D. the breakdown of any structure or foundation supporting the object

    5.___

6. Homeowners' policies often contain a provision of coverage for the replacement value of personal property by endorsement.
Which of the following is NOT typical of such a provision?

    A. It does not apply to property not being used or stored by the insured.
    B. It does not apply to property which cannot be replaced.
    C. The insured may make a claim on the endorsement within 180 days of having refused to make such a claim.
    D. The insurer is not liable until repairs or replacements are carried out.

    6.___

7. The time element used in the calculation of business interruption loss continues until 7._____

   A. sales return to volume experienced before loss occurred
   B. property is restored so that insured can resume partial operation
   C. end of time it would take to repair or replace damaged property
   D. insured has exhausted all coverage granted by his/her policy

8. Which of the following is a type of multiple-line policy that provides all risk coverage to manufacturers on personal property away from the premises? 8._____

   A. HPR   B. MOP   C. SMP   D. PIP

9. A fire is started in a part of a building that is outside the boundaries of the insured's property, and then spreads. The insured's property is damaged, and a claim is filed. The fire's origin would be described in the claim as being. 9._____

   A. extended   B. off premises
   C. on premises   D. communicated

10. In order to calculate the cost of goods sold for a business interruption loss, an adjuster should determine 10._____

    A. purchases for a specific period of time
    B. beginning and ending inventory for a specific period of time
    C. gross sales for a specific period of time, using business receipts provided by the insured
    D. beginning and ending inventory and purchases for a specific period of time

11. After a business interruption loss, the insured is able to continue in business, but because a part of the stock is damaged, the suspension will only be partial. The insured should be advised to 11._____

    A. close his books on the date of the loss
    B. sell his stock and receive reimbursement for a full suspension of business
    C. close his books on the date of the loss and then reopen them after the suspension period has ended
    D. close his books on the date of the loss and then reopen them for the period of suspension

12. How should a manufacturing policy with an *ordinary payroll endorsement* form attached to it be handled when determining the gross earnings value for a business interruption claim? 12._____

    A. Direct or productive payroll is deducted from gross earnings loss, along with direct labor and cost of goods sold.
    B. An *ordinary payroll endorsement* form has no effect on gross earnings value.
    C. Direct or productive payroll is added to sales value of production along with cost of goods sold.
    D. Direct or productive payroll is deducted from sales value of production along with cost of goods sold.

13. Clauses naming or designating payees are either mortgagee or _____ clauses. 13._____

    A. loss   B. liberalization
    C. subrogation   D. loss payable

14. The replacement cost coverage of most building policies provides that the insured may elect to be paid the actual cash value of the repairs or replacements, and within _____ days make a claim for the portion due under replacement cost coverage.

    A. 30 B. 60 C. 180 D. 360

15. Policies which describe property and add clauses limiting the extent of the application of the insurance in case of loss are known as _____ policies.

    A. excess
    C. contribution
    B. coinsurance
    D. restricted

16. A person who is suing the insured, or holds a judgment, and is seeking to satisfy the claim out of the proceeds of insurance is called a(n)

    A. bailee
    C. garnishee
    B. assignee
    D. lessor

17. How does an agreed amount endorsement affect a basic business interruption policy?

    A. Suspends application of the coinsurance clause
    B. Extends limit of liability beyond the date it would take to restore facilities
    C. Provides coverage to insured for loss caused by inability of supplier to provide goods or services because of loss at suppliers' premises
    D. Provides coverage for extra expense necessary to continue business in a manner similar to that prior to loss

18. What is the term used to describe something installed or placed on an insured's premises for the purpose of conducting business?

    A. Trade fixture
    C. Display
    B. Bonded commercial risk
    D. Mercantile annex

19. To provide that there shall be no liability for the insurer unless loss exceeds a stipulated amount or a stipulated percentage of the value involved in a loss, _____ clauses are sometimes added to policies.

    A. deductible
    C. liberalization clauses
    B. franchise
    D. excess

20. The entity whose performance is being guaranteed in suretyship is known as the

    A. primary beneficiary
    C. principal
    B. fiduciary
    D. insurer

21. A(n) _____ loss is NOT directly caused by damage to property, but arises as a result of such damage.

    A. proximate
    C. end
    B. commuted
    D. consequential

22. Coverage for losses that are detected during the term of a reinsurance treaty, regardless of when they were sustained, is known as _____ coverage.

    A. extended
    C. retroactive
    B. discovery
    D. redundant

23. Under the typical provisions of a standard homeowners policy, assuming that each loss is caused by a vehicle not owned or operated by any occupant of the premises, which of the following vehicle losses would be covered?   23._____
    A. Clothing of a passenger is torn by catching on projection in or on a stationary vehicle.
    B. Rain or snow damages contents of a vehicle because windows leak.
    C. Insured's fragile article damaged when struck against part of a stationary vehicle.
    D. Insured's furniture is thrown from a vehicle as a result of an accident.

24. After a business interruption loss, the insured is unable to obtain and assemble all of the necessary figures to present and verify claim without incurring considerable expense. The insured _____ include this expense as part of his claim, _____.   24._____
    A. may or may not; depending on the conditions of each policy
    B. may not; because the policy conditions state that presentation and verification of claim are his obligations
    C. may; because presentation and verification of claim are obligations created as a direct result of the damage incurred.
    D. may; so long as the insured can prove that the presentation and verification of claim are a direct result of the damage incurred

25. In reference to windstorm and hail, MOST broad form homeowners policies include loss   25._____
    A. caused directly or indirectly by frost, cold weather, or ice
    B. the collapse of an insured structure, which collapse is directly caused by a windstorm
    C. to watercraft that are not stored inside the home
    D. the interior of the building if damaged by rain entering an opening not previously caused by wind or hail

KEY (CORRECT ANSWERS)

1.	C	11.	D
2.	B	12.	D
3.	B	13.	D
4.	C	14.	C
5.	B	15.	A
6.	C	16.	C
7.	C	17.	A
8.	B	18.	A
9.	D	19.	B
10.	D	20.	C

21.	D
22.	B
23.	D
24.	B
25.	B

EXAMINATION SECTION
TEST 1

DIRECTIONS: Each question or incomplete statement is followed by several suggested answers or completions. Select the one that BEST answers the question or completes the Statement. *PRINT THE LETTER OF THE CORRECT ANSWER IN THE SPACE AT THE RIGHT.*

1. Pure risk exists when

    A. there is only the probability of loss
    B. the insured decides how much risk to assume
    C. there is the possibility of loss or gain
    D. there is risk of loss
    E. risk is certain

2. Protection is needed as long as

    A. there is exposure
    B. the possibility of loss exists
    C. the potential of risk exists
    D. the possibility of risk exists
    E. there is value

3. What type of insurer collected the HIGHEST percent of all property and liability insurance premiums?

    A. Reciprocals   B. Mutual companies
    C. Individuals   D. Stock companies
    E. Lloyds Groups

4. The LEAST important consideration in choosing an insurer should be

    A. field of specialization   B. financial stability
    C. coverage   D. flexibility
    E. cost of coverage

5. Employers are NOT required to carry workmen's compensation insurance when they

    A. have only a few workers
    B. have only part-time workers
    C. carry health and life insurance for employees
    D. are not engaged in hazardous jobs
    E. are the sole employees

6. An insurer may void a contract when

    A. there is only oral representation
    B. the representation is based on fact or opinion
    C. the insured purposefully concealed significant information essential to the risk
    D. a misrepresentation is not material to the risk
    E. all of the above

71

7. What type of insurance contract is NOT cancellable once it is in force?

   A. Property   B. Life   C. Accident
   D. Health   E. All of the above

8. What type of insurance is NOT considered a contract of indemnity?

   A. Life   B. Health   C. Property
   D. Liability   E. Fire

9. Deductibles serve *mainly* to
   I. discourage over-insurance
   II. allow the insurer to escape its rightful obligations
   III. exclude small losses
   IV. permit the insured to bear part of the loss in return for premium reduction
   V. exclude frequent losses

   The CORRECT answer is:

   A. II, III, IV   B. I, IV   C. II, III, V
   D. I, II, IV   E. I, II, III, IV, V

10. An attachment in a fire insurance policy which describes the insured property is called the

    A. blanket   B. insuring clause
    C. endorsement   D. form
    E. core

11. Cities are rated for fire insurance according to all of the following criteria EXCEPT:

    A. Adequacy of water supply   B. Fire departments
    C. Alarm systems   D. Structural conditions
    E. Population

12. What type of losses do MOST liability policies cover?
    I. Costs of defending suits alleging bodily injury or property damage
    II. Expenses incurred in the investigation, defense or settlement of an accident
    III. Legally obligated sums payable because of bodily injury or damage to property of others
    IV. Damage to property of others which is in the business's care, custody or control
    V. Obligations under Workers' Compensation laws

    The CORRECT answer is:

    A. I, III, IV   B. I, II, III   C. III, IV, V
    D. III, IV   E. I, II, III, IV, V

13. An employer is held liable when an employee is at fault in an accident while

    A. using his own car on behalf of the employer
    B. operating a car belonging to customers
    C. operating a rented car on behalf of the employer
    D. operating the leased car of the business
    E. all of the above

14. The *average* rate paid for the loss of use of a stolen car covered by theft insurance is closest to _____ per day.

    A. $20   B. $50   C. $65   D. $80   E. $100

15. According to common law, an employer has all of the following duties EXCEPT to

    A. protect his employees from theft
    B. hire competent fellow employees
    C. warn his employees of any existing danger
    D. provide safe tools
    E. provide his employees with a safe place to work

16. What kind of benefits are usually covered under workmen's compensation policies?
    I. Medical care to the injured workmen
    II. Lump sums for dismemberment and death
    III. Benefits for disablements by occupational disease
    IV. Benefits for mental anguish and loss of consortium
    V. Income payments for life

    The CORRECT answer is:

    A. I, II, V   B. I, II, III   C. I, II, IV, V
    D. I, II   E. I, II, III, IV, V

17. Burglary insurance covers

    A. all stolen property from the premises
    B. all stolen property on or off the premises
    C. stolen property when there are visible marks of forced entry
    D. stolen property when the thief can be identified
    E. property stolen by an "outsider"

18. The "Fair Plan Program" is intended for businesses

    A. in high-risk areas
    B. that are high-risk types
    C. with over a certain number of employees
    D. cooperating with agencies to hire the unemployable
    E. with high claim records

19. Disability insurance is *particularly* appropriate when

    A. the company is small
    B. the business owner's insurance is not in force
    C. group coverage is not in force
    D. the company is large
    E. the occupation is hazardous

20. The MOST indispensable part of a business continuation plan is

    A. life insurance
    B. an entity plan
    C. a cross-purchase plan
    D. key man coverage
    E. purchase and sale agreement

21. The general reliability of insurers is rated by

    A. the insurance commissioner of each state
    B. Charteree Underwriter Guide
    C. The American College of Life Underwriters
    D. Best's Insurance Reports
    E. M.I.G. (Master Insurance Guide)

22. The MAIN value of insurance is to

    A. reduce worry
    B. stimulate initiative
    C. reduce pure risk
    D. transfer risk
    E. prevent loss

23. Noninsurance should be restricted to all of the following circumstances EXCEPT where the

    A. severity of the potential loss is low
    B. risks are more or less predictable
    C. risks are preventable
    D. risks are largely reducible
    E. risks are narrowly diversified

24. Insurers composed of groups of individual underwriters are called

    A. self-insurers
    B. reciprocals
    C. stock companies
    D. mutual companies
    E. Lloyds groups

25. What types of insurers dominate the life insurance field?
    I. Self-insurers
    II. Reciprocals
    III. Lloyds groups
    IV. Mutual companies
    V. Stock companies

    The CORRECT answer is:

    A. I, II, IV
    B. I, III, V
    C. IV, V
    D. I, V
    E. II, V

26. The direct writing system is traditionally used for _____ insurance.

    A. fire
    B. liability
    C. life
    D. workers' compensation
    E. property

27. Local agents are generally NOT authorized to bind insurance

    A. orally
    B. over the telephone
    C. up to certain limits
    D. on certain kinds of property
    E. on all types they sell

28. The *only* type of insurance which does not require an insurable interest to exist at the time of loss is

   A. property   B. liability   C. fire
   D. life   E. none of the above

29. Subrogation allows the

   A. insured to recover from a liable third party
   B. insurer to recover from a liable third party
   C. insured to recover from the insurer and liable third party
   D. insurer to escape its rightful obligations
   E. liable third parties to escape their obligations

30. If a person negligently takes the life of the insured

   A. the insurer may proceed against the negligent third party
   B. the insurer is not obligated to pay the face value of the policy
   C. representatives of the insured may collect the face value of the policy and proceed against the negligent third party
   D. representatives of the insured party may only collect the face value of the policy
   E. representatives of the insured party may collect premiums the insured has paid and proceed against the negligent third party

31. Coinsurance

   A. discourages overinsurance
   B. discourages underinsurance
   C. causes the insured to assume part of the loss
   D. excludes certain perils from coverage
   E. reinforces the indemnity principle

32. What percent of the fire insurance premium is refunded when a one year policy is cancelled at six months by the insured?

   A. 50   B. 45   C. 40   D. 30   E. 0

33. When a customer falls on a slippery floor in an area where there are signs clearly warning of the danger it is

   A. actionable negligence, unintentional in nature
   B. actionable negligence, intentional in nature
   C. contributory negligence
   D. accidental negligence
   E. non-negligent

34. Liability rates are *usually* based upon

   A. front footages
   B. sales volume
   C. admissions
   D. loss experience in given territories
   E. floor area

35. An automobile comprehensive policy does NOT exclude losses from

    A. wear and tear
    B. mechanical breakdown resulting from theft
    C. radioactive contamination
    D. freezing
    E. all of the above

36. The employer's common law defense asserting that the employee knowingly assumed certain risks when he accepted employment is called

    A. contributory negligence   B. unintentional negligence
    C. primary commercial blanket   D. assumption of risk
    E. blanket position

37. Which of the following types of employment is not covered by workmen's compensation law in MOST states?

    A. Agricultural   B. Casual
    C. Domestic   D. All of the above
    E. None of the above

38. The MAIN advantage of a blanket fidelity bond is that

    A. the discovery period is two years
    B. theft is covered even if the thief is unknown
    C. the limit of loss is reinstated to the full amount after each loss
    D. each employee is covered up to the limit of the bond
    E. positions, not individual employees, are covered

39. Major medical plans

    A. pay costs of hospitalization, medication and medical care
    B. pay the complete cost of certain described hospital care
    C. pay a stated proportion of an employee's annual salary should he suffer a long-term physical disability
    D. attempt to meet the cost of catastrophic illnesses
    E. eliminate the substantial deductibles of basic medical plans

40. What type of insurance policy is designed to assure the continuation of a business following the premature death of an owner?

    A. Business Owners'   B. Key-Man
    C. Term Life   D. Disability
    E. Trust

41. The insurance proceeds in purchase and sale agreements are *usually* paid to

    A. the surviving partners
    B. a trustee
    C. the business
    D. the estate of the deceased
    E. the surviving parties to the agreement

42. The determination of a loss as trivial hinges on the 42.____

    A. probability of the loss
    B. amount of the loss
    C. severity of the loss
    D. exposure of the loss
    E. financial resources of the business

43. The risk transfer method of reducing business risks involve 43.____

    A. loss prevention programs
    B. the lease device
    C. purchasing coverage
    D. separate and distinct funds set aside for this purpose
    E. trivial loss

44. The designation "C.P.C.U." indicates that the insurance agent 44.____

    A. is a competent, professional person and interested in his work
    B. can obtain insurance even for unusual exposure and risk
    C. is able to recommend what constitutes an adequate insurance program
    D. has a college degree
    E. has a clean record, a certain number of years of experience, and volume of sales

45. Dwarf is the owner of a building and holds property insurance on it naming himself as the insured. Later the building is sold to Gupta and the policy is left unchanged. The building is destroyed by fire. 45.____
    The insurance proceeds, in this case, would be paid to

    A. Dwarf
    B. Gupta
    C. Dwarf or Gupta
    D. half to Dwarf and half to Gupta
    E. neither Dwarf nor Gupta

46. Insurance companies solve the problem of some persons carrying full insurance to value and others not carrying full insurance to value by 46.____

    A. requiring a high deductible
    B. changing a differential
    C. raising premiums
    D. requiring annual appraisals
    E. using the coinsurance clause

47. The standard fire policy, excluding endorsements, insures for 47.____
    I. fire
    II. lightning
    III. windstorm
    IV. smoke damage
    V. losses to goods temporarily removed from the premises because of a fire
    The CORRECT answer is:

    A. I, II, V   B. I, II, IV   C. I, II, III
    D. I, IV, V   E. I, II, III, IV, V

48. The basic fire policy limits coverage to trees, shrubs, and lawns to _____ per cent.

    A. 0   B. 1   C. 2   D. 4   E. 5

49. Which incident below would be FULLY covered by a liability policy containing a $100,000 limit per person injured, or a total of $300,000 in any one accident?

    A. Two persons injured in a single accident awarded judgments of $150,000 each
    B. Ten persons injured in a single accident awarded judgments totalling $350,000
    C. Three persons injured in a single accident awarded judgments of $300,000 each
    D. One person injured in a single accident awarded a judgment of $300,000
    E. Ten people injured in a single accident awarded judgments of $30,000 each

50. Automobile collision insurance policies cover

    A. glass breakage
    B. damage from malicious mishcief and vandalism
    C. damage from falling objects
    D. damage from windstorm
    E. none of the above

KEY (CORRECT ANSWERS)

1. A	11. E	21. D	31. B	41. B
2. D	12. B	22. C	32. C	42. E
3. D	13. E	23. E	33. A	43. B
4. E	14. B	24. E	34. E	44. A
5. E	15. A	25. C	35. B	45. E
6. C	16. B	26. C	36. D	46. E
7. B	17. C	27. E	37. D	47. A
8. A	18. A	28. D	38. B	48. E
9. B	19. C	29. B	39. D	49. E
10. D	20. E	30. C	40. A	50. E

EXAMINATION SECTION
TEST 1

DIRECTIONS: Each question or incomplete statement is followed by several suggested answers or completions. Select the one that BEST answers the question or completes the statement. *PRINT THE LETTER OF THE CORRECT ANSWER IN THE SPACE AT THE RIGHT.*

1. A retail merchant who loses profits because of a fire that ruins his/her stock would have this loss covered under a(n) _____ policy.

   A. accounts receivable
   B. leasehold
   C. profits and commissions
   D. business interruption

2. Each of the following is an *allied line* type of insurance policy EXCEPT

   A. sprinkler leakage
   B. rain
   C. explosion
   D. water damage

3. The concept of *excess insurance* applies to casualty insurance in terms of

   A. heavy financing plans such as mortgages
   B. the assumption of liability by overlapping policies
   C. liability for coverage amounts excluded in a three-fourths value clause
   D. adverse selection during the underwriting process

4. Under the standard fire policy, an insured may file suit against the insurer only if the suit is filed within _____ of the loss.

   A. 30 days   B. 90 days   C. 1 year   D. 2 years

5. A person who is held to be liable for another person's bodily injury may have to compensate the injury for *special damages.*
   Which of the following is NOT an example of special damages?

   A. Lost income
   B. Mental suffering
   C. Rehabilitation expenses
   D. Physicians' fees

6. With an additional premium charge, _____ can be insured on an owners', landlords', and tenants' policy.

   A. agents for owners of the managed property
   B. executives of an insured corporation
   C. tenants
   D. mortgagees

7. The three broad areas of liability include each of the following EXCEPT

   A. business
   B. professional
   C. assumed
   D. personal

8. An insured has a provisional reporting fire policy. After reporting a value of $100,000, the insured suffers a $50,000 loss. However, the true value is found to have been $125,000 at the time of reporting.
   The policy will pay

   A. $25,000   B. $35,000   C. $40,000   D. $50,000

9. Of the following types of policies, _____ liability is NOT divided into separate coverages for bodily injury liability and property damage liability.

   A. storekeepers'
   B. comprehensive general
   C. products
   D. contractual

10. For a loss to come within the coverage of a basic mercantile open stock burglary policy, all of the following conditions must be met EXCEPT

   A. premises must be closed
   B. entry and exit must be made by force
   C. interior rooms are forcibly entered after a non-forced entry onto premises
   D. marks of violence must be left on premises at the place of entry or exit

11. In terms of property insurance, which of the following is NOT a *broad form* peril?

   A. Glass breakage
   B. Falling objects
   C. Volcanic activity
   D. Water damage

12. Without endorsement, the standard fire policy

   A. covers lightning damage
   B. does not permit other insurance
   C. requires a pro rata premium return from the insurer if the insured cancels
   D. prohibits asset mortgages

13. If notice is given within _____ days prior to an associated loss, there will be automatic coverage for additional premises that are acquired under an owners', landlords', and tenants' policy.

   A. 8   B. 15   C. 30   D. 60

14. A paymaster robbery policy covers money and checks intended for payroll

   A. along with the money and checks constituting a single day's deposit
   B. along with securities intended for pension and health plans
   C. along with money and checks for deposit, and pension and health securities of the insured *only*

15. Individuals and businesses face three basic types of liability exposures. Which of the following is NOT one of these three?

   A. Automobile
   B. General
   C. Fiduciary
   D. Employers'

16. A workers' compensation policy may NOT be canceled by an insurer

   A. on a short rate basis for the time the insurance was in force
   B. in accordance with the terms of the policy
   C. on a short rate basis if the insured requests cancellation because of retirement
   D. on the basis of a charge of the minimum specified premium if the final premium computed is less than the minimum premium

17. A person has two separate owners', landlords', and tenants' policies, covering the same losses. Company X's policy has bodily injury limits of $10,000/$20,000, and Company Y's policy covers up to $20,000/$40,000.
    If a proper claim of $6,000 is filed, Company

    A. X will pay $2,000
    B. X will pay nothing
    C. Y will pay $3,000
    D. X will pay $2,000

18. A customer enters a store owned by a public liability policyholder, falls, and injures himself. The policy has no endorsement.
    In order for the injured party to collect damages from the insurer, it is necessary that the injury be proven to be the result of the owner's negligence, OR that the

    A. owner carries a personal comprehensive policy
    B. injury results in death
    C. policy has a medical payments endorsement
    D. injury is the result of a malicious act by another customer in the store

19. In broad terms, an owners', landlords', and tenants' policy covers

    A. use, ownership or maintenance of premises
    B. completed operations
    C. use, ownership or maintenance of buildings or vehicles
    D. products

20. Which of the following property is excluded from the basic dwelling form of a fire insurance policy?

    A. Trees, shrubs, plants, and lawn
    B. Materials and supplies on or adjacent to the premises used to make alterations
    C. Fixtures owned by the insured and pertaining to the service of the premises
    D. Private structures for use with the dwelling and located on the premises

21. All of the following are excluded from a basic mercantile safe burglary policy EXCEPT

    A. manuscripts
    B. securities
    C. records
    D. accounts

22. The broad form of the storekeepers' burglary and robbery policy is USUALLY available only to single-location risks which do not employ more than _____ persons.

    A. 2   B. 4   C. 10   D. 12

23. Umbrella liability insurance is considered *excess* insurance in three respects.
    Which of the following is NOT one of these?

    A. Provides automatic replacement for existing coverages exhausted or reduced by loss
    B. Is often accountable for overinsurance in cases of workers' compensation
    C. Covers exposures not otherwise covered
    D. Provides higher limits than the other coverages owned

24. A collision automobile policy covers damage caused by

    A. falling aircraft parts
    B. a falling tree
    C. falling rock
    D. upset

25. Which of the following liability exposures is USUALLY excluded from, but may be written in combination with, a comprehensive general liability policy? 25.___

    A. Products and completed operations
    B. Workers' compensation
    C. Structural alterations
    D. Automobile

KEY (CORRECT ANSWERS)

1.	D	11.	C
2.	C	12.	A
3.	B	13.	B
4.	C	14.	D
5.	B	15.	C
6.	C	16.	C
7.	C	17.	D
8.	C	18.	C
9.	A	19.	A
10.	C	20.	A

    21. B
    22. B
    23. B
    24. D
    25. D

TEST 2

DIRECTIONS: Each question or incomplete statement is followed by several suggested answers or completions. Select the one that BEST answers the question or completes the statement. *PRINT THE LETTER OF THE CORRECT ANSWER IN THE SPACE AT THE RIGHT.*

1. Which of the following is NOT an optional coverage under a garage liability policy?   1.____

   A. Cars leased--insured lessor
   B. Legal liability
   C. Medical
   D. Legal

2. Which of the following professionals would have the LEAST need for professional liability coverage?   2.____

   A. Architect
   B. Insurance agent
   C. Building contractor
   D. Actuary

3. A small-business boiler and machinery policy may be written for a   3.____

   A. laundry
   B. restaurant
   C. hospital
   D. greenhouse

4. In order to be covered by a worker's compensation policy, _____ must be specifically named in the policy.   4.____

   A. watchmen
   B. relatives of the employer
   C. part-time employees
   D. outside workers such as contractors

Questions 5-7.

DIRECTIONS: Questions 5 through 7 are to be answered on the basis of the following information.

Mr. Stark owns three buildings. Building A is worth $50,000, Building B is worth $30,000, and Building C is worth $20,000. He insures all three in a blanket policy, which includes a distribution clause, for $50,000.

5. In the event of a total loss to Building A, how much will the insurer pay?   5.____

   A. $10,000   B. $15,000   C. $25,000   D. $30,000

6. In the event of a $20,000 fire loss to Building A, the insurer will pay   6.____

   A. $2,500   B. $10,000   C. $15,000   D. $20,000

7. In the event of a $15,000 loss to Building C, how much will the insurer pay?   7.____

   A. $5,000   B. $7,500   C. $10,000   D. $15,000

8. Which of the following losses would be covered by a standard boiler and machinery policy?

   A. Deformation caused by water or steam pressure
   B. Corrosion of metal parts
   C. Explosion of gas in furnace
   D. Collapse of furnace

9. All of the following are *usually* covered under a typical glass insurance policy EXCEPT

   A. glass damage caused by fire
   B. repair of frames
   C. malicious application of chemicals
   D. unexplained breakage

10. The rates for Coverage A of a money and securities broad form policy are based on all of the following factors EXCEPT

    A. insured's occupation
    B. type of safe or vault on insured's premises
    C. territory in which insured's premises are located
    D. number of guards employed to accompany messengers

11. Each of the following is a type of coverage that can be added by endorsement to the comprehensive general liability policy EXCEPT

    A. incidental medical malpractice
    B. nonowned watercraft liability
    C. products liability--completed operations
    D. limited worldwide coverage

12. Which of the following is NOT a type of Fidelity Bond?

    A. Plumbers
    B. Bankers blanket
    C. Primary blanket
    D. Blanket position

13. The coinsurance percentage of a mercantile open stock policy's coinsurance clause is determined by

    A. type of merchandise
    B. business frontage
    C. territory
    D. per unit cost

14. All of the following are excluded from the personal injury coverage of a public liability policy EXCEPT liability

    A. assumed under any contract
    B. assumed in any forum of the public media
    C. of an employer to an employee which arises out of the employment
    D. arising out of willful violation of a statute with the insured's knowledge

15. Under the extended coverage endorsement of a standard fire policy, _____ explosion is covered.

    A. water heater
    B. gas
    C. flywheel
    D. steam boiler

16. During construction operations, an employee of a subcontractor drops an object on one of the general contractor's employees.
    What kind of policy would protect the general contractor from this loss?

    A. Worker's compensation
    B. Subcontractors
    C. Manufacturers and contractors
    D. Comprehensive personal

    16.____

17. An average clause assures that

    A. the insured will keep insurance that is at least equal to a certain percentage of the property value at the time of loss
    B. no more than the average clause percentage of a loss will be paid
    C. no more than the average clause percentage can be applied to cover the loss of any one building
    D. the insured will report the true property value every month

    17.____

18. Which of the following is covered under the basic mercantile open stock burglary policy?

    A. Fur articles
    B. Vandalism and malicious mischief
    C. Exterior damage caused by forcible entry
    D. Nuclear perils

    18.____

19. The purpose of a cracked glass endorsement in a glass insurance policy is to

    A. specifically exclude all types of glass cracks from coverage
    B. include certain types of cracks in the coverage
    C. include coverage of glass cracked by heat from fire only
    D. relieve the insurer of liability for the extension of cracks existing at the time of application

    19.____

20. Which of the following is covered by a miscellaneous liability policy?

    A. Operation of automobiles
    B. Damage to property owned by the insured
    C. Operation of aircraft
    D. Bodily injury liability

    20.____

21. An owners', landlords', and tenants' policy defines all of the following as *mobile equipment* EXCEPT

    A. vehicles not subject to motor vehicle registration
    B. vehicles leased exclusively by the insured, solely for use on insured premises
    C. loaders
    D. vehicles maintained exclusively on premises owned by the insured

    21.____

22. Which of the following can be covered by water damage insurance?

    A. Water seeping through building walls
    B. Legal liability
    C. Leaking plumbing
    D. Assumed liability

    22.____

23. A basic personal theft policy can be written as an endorsement on a(n) _____ insurance policy.

    A. open stock burglary
    B. personal property
    C. flood
    D. fire

24. Which of the following statements about glass insurance is FALSE?

    A. Salvage belongs to the insurer.
    B. The insured pays half of each loss under the retention of 50-50 coverage.
    C. Scratches are not covered.
    D. Residential policies do not describe every single piece covered.

25. Coverage C of the general property form of fire insurance covers

    A. personal property owned by others
    B. business personal property
    C. attached additions
    D. equipment permanently a part of the building and used in its service

---

KEY (CORRECT ANSWERS)

1. A		11. C
2. C		12. A
3. B		13. C
4. B		14. B
5. C		15. B
6. B		16. A
7. B		17. A
8. C		18. C
9. A		19. D
10. D		20. D

21. B
22. A
23. D
24. B
25. A

TEST 3

DIRECTIONS: Each question or incomplete statement is followed by several suggested answers or completions. Select the one that BEST answers the question or completes the statement. *PRINT THE LETTER OF THE CORRECT ANSWER IN THE SPACE AT THE RIGHT.*

1. In order to be covered by workers compensation, an injury must 1.____

    A. be due to the employer's negligence
    B. arise out of, but not necessarily be suffered in the course of, employment
    C. cause a time of loss and physical impairment
    D. arise out of and be suffered in the course of employment

2. All of the following are *usually* excluded from a broad form personal theft policy EXCEPT 2.____

    A. animals
    B. depositories
    C. trailers
    D. carpet samples

3. Which of the following statements about glass insurance is TRUE? 3.____

    A. Lettering on glass is not covered.
    B. Scratches are covered.
    C. All risk coverage for neon signs may be added by endorsement.
    D. The cost of removing and replacing window displays that are displaced during repair is included.

4. In the case of an adjustment dispute, how many appraisers are USUALLY chosen to settle the value of the damaged property covered by a standard fire policy? 4.____

    A. One
    B. Two
    C. Three
    D. Number is dependent on the policy

5. Of the following, _____ is covered by a Money and Securities Broad Form policy. 5.____

    A. employee theft or embezzlement
    B. surrender of money in an exchange
    C. loss of money by fire
    D. destruction of assets by war

6. A written agreement, signed by both parties, in which the claimant in a liability suit agrees to drop his/her claim, and the policyholder, through the insurer, agrees to pay the agreed amount is called a 6.____

    A. resolution
    B. release
    C. representation
    D. settlement

7. Under the extended coverage endorsement of a standard fire policy, a _____ is covered. 7.____

    A. steam pipe explosion
    B. rain damage to rugs, from a window left open

87

C. damage to fence by a neighbor's car
D. wind damage to an awning

8. If a restaurant owner is sued because a customer got sick from eating a meal served at the restaurant, the owner would be covered under a(n) _____ policy.

    A. products
    B. completed operations
    C. owners', landlords', and tenants'
    D. personal comprehensive

9. An aviation accident policy covers losses caused by

    A. racing
    B. aircraft collision
    C. crop dusting
    D. aerial photography

10. Under a mercantile robbery policy, rates for interior robbery insurance are based on all of the following factors EXCEPT

    A. the insured's business
    B. type of safe or vault
    C. the territory in which the risk is located
    D. the number of custodians on duty

11. Which of the following is excluded from a typical garage liability policy?

    A. Automobile rented to others
    B. Property damage
    C. Bodily injury
    D. Use of owned and non-owned cars

12. The paymaster robbery broad form policy adds all of the following to basic coverage EXCEPT

    A. mysterious disappearance
    B. dishonesty of employees
    C. wrongful abstraction
    D. actual destruction

13. Which of the following is NOT included in a fiduciary bond?

    A. Receiver
    B. Executor
    C. Attachment
    D. Administrator

14. Cash benefits for workers' compensation include all of the following EXCEPT

    A. survivor
    B. disability
    C. impairment
    D. rehabilitation

15. An owners', landlords', and tenants' policy covering the property owner will cover

    A. damage to an item owned by the insured
    B. damage to an item borrowed by the insured
    C. injury to a tenant
    D. injury to an employee covered by worker's compensation

16. Which of the following is NOT a general crime exclusion contained in business crime coverage?   16._____

    A. Vandalism   B. Fixtures
    C. Employee dishonesty   D. Ornamentation

17. Mr. Langley has an automobile policy with bodily injury liability limits of $30,000/$60,000.   17._____
    He later injured a person in an accident, and the injured person received a $12,000 judgment against Mr. Langley. The court costs amount to $2,000, and Mr. Langley or his insurance company has to pay them. The fee for the attorney who represented Mr. Langley was $10,000.
    How much of all of these costs will Mr. Langley's insurance pay?

    A. $12,000   B. $14,000   C. $22,000   D. $24,000

18. Following the loss of a burglary directed at an insured's safe, which of the following would   18._____
    NOT be covered under a basic mercantile safe burglary policy?

    A. Damage to fixtures outside safe
    B. Theft of securities held outside safe
    C. Damage to building containing safe
    D. Burglary through manipulation of combination lock

19. In order for a loss to be covered under a money and securities broad form policy, a loss   19._____
    must occur while the policy is in force, and must be discovered within _____ after the policy has been terminated.

    A. 90 days   B. 180 days   C. 1 year   D. 2 years

20. For which policies are 50% retentions sometimes written?   20._____

    A. Boiler and machinery
    B. Owners', landlords', and tenants'
    C. Glass
    D. Workers', compensation

21. The paymaster robbery form covers the payroll from the time it is   21._____

    A. delivered to the employer until it is deposited by each worker
    B. delivered to the employer until the workers are paid
    C. drawn from the bank until the workers are paid
    D. drawn from the bank until 12 hours following the official end of the pay period

22. When a miscellaneous liability policy is written on an estimated premium basis, the   22._____
    insured must keep his/her books and records available for review for a period of _____ after the policy has expired.

    A. 90 days   B. 180 days   C. 1 year   D. 2 years

23. Under a basic storekeepers' burglary and robbery policy, each of the following is covered   23._____
    EXCEPT

    A. safe burglary
    B. embezzlement
    C. damage to property and premises
    D. kidnapping

24. A contractor builds a house that later falls in after it is finished due to poor construction. The homeowner is hurt in the collapse and sues the contractor.
Under what kind of policy would the contractor be protected?

    A. Owners', landlords', and tenants'
    B. Completed operations
    C. Manufacturers and contractors
    D. Products

25. Under a messenger robbery policy, a guard accompanying the messenger must be a male person of AT LEAST _____ years of age.

    A. 17   B. 19   C. 21   D. 23

KEY (CORRECT ANSWERS)

1.	D	11.	A
2.	B	12.	B
3.	C	13.	C
4.	C	14.	D
5.	C	15.	C
6.	B	16.	B
7.	D	17.	D
8.	A	18.	D
9.	B	19.	C
10.	B	20.	C

21. C
22. C
23. B
24. B
25. A

TEST 4

DIRECTIONS: Each question or incomplete statement is followed by several suggested answers or completions. Select the one that BEST answers the question or completes the statement. *PRINT THE LETTER OF THE CORRECT ANSWER IN THE SPACE AT THE RIGHT.*

1. A dwelling form of a fire insurance policy permits the insured to apply up to _____ % of the amount of insurance on the dwelling to cover any other private structure and garage on the premises whose use is incidental to the maintenance of the main building.

    A. 10 B. 25 C. 35 D. 50

2. Which of the following is NOT covered under the *comprehensive* part of an automobile policy?

    A. Windstorm B. Collision C. Theft D. Fire

3. If a personal theft policy is written with divided coverage, what kind of property is insured for a different amount from all other types of property?

    A. Money and securities
    B. Art objects
    C. Jewelry and furs
    D. Irreplaceable objects

4. Under the broad form personal theft policy, what coverage is added to the basic policy?

    A. Depositories
    B. Vandalism and malicious mischief
    C. Warehouses
    D. Mysterious disappearance

5. If a dwelling and contents endorsement is added to a standard fire policy, _____ will be excluded from coverage.

    A. pictures and books
    B. deeds and accounts
    C. bills and currency
    D. money and securities

6. The consequential damage endorsement to a boiler and machinery policy is written PRIMARILY to cover

    A. freezing caused by exposure suffered as a result of an explosion or malfunction
    B. losses due to fire caused by explosion
    C. product contamination
    D. product spoilage

7. The extended coverage endorsement to the standard fire policy excludes the peril of

    A. water damage
    B. riot and civil commotion
    C. explosion
    D. aircraft

8. Ms. Singer, a businessowner, has a provisional reporting fire policy on her stock. At the end of one month she has $96,000 of stock on hand. However, she has anticipated selling most of it quickly, and reports a value of $48,000.
   If she then suffers a $20,000 loss, how much will the company pay?

    A. $5,000 B. $10,000 C. $15,000 D. $20,000

9. Each of the following is an example of *personal injury* EXCEPT

   A. invasion of privacy
   B. discrimination
   C. assault
   D. defamation

10. Manufacturers' and contractors' liability policies are USUALLY rated on a(n) _____.

    A. payroll
    B. hours worked
    C. net receipts
    D. area of premises

11. General liability policies are USUALLY written on a _____ basis.

    A. claims-made
    B. scaled
    C. claims occurrence
    D. discovery

12. Under the broad form of a storekeepers burglary and robbery policy, what coverage is added to the basic policy?

    A. Theft of night depository
    B. Kidnapping
    C. Safe burglary
    D. Employee dishonesty

13. The pair and set clause of a broad form personal theft policy stipulates that

    A. the policy will consider the loss of one item from a pair or set to be a total loss
    B. the loss of any item in a pair or set will be indemnified on a strict pro rata basis
    C. the policy will give consideration to the importance of an item which is lost from a pair or set, but the loss will not be considered total
    D. a loss is not subject to indemnity unless all items in a pair or set are lost

14. Which of the following is NOT covered by a standard water damage policy?

    A. Sewer backup
    B. Rain/snow damage
    C. Plumbing leaks
    D. Business interruption

15. Liability exposure created by new construction and demolition operations will be unconditionally covered under the _____ form.

    A. owners', landlords', and tenants'
    B. manufacturers' and contractors'
    C. comprehensive general liability
    D. none of the above

16. If an insured owns a $100,000 building that is covered by a $40,000 policy with an 80% average clause, how much would the insurer pay in the case of a $20,000 loss?

    A. $10,000   B. $16,000   C. $20,000   D. $32,000

17. When adjusting a glass insurance loss, it is necessary to measure each pane of glass

    A. under any circumstances
    B. under no circumstances
    C. for a residential loss only
    D. for a business loss only

18. A person who is held to be liable for another person's bodily injury may have to compen- 18.____
sate the injury for *general damages.*
Which of the following is NOT an example of general damages?

    A. Permanent injury   B. Loss of time
    C. Loss of consortium   D. Pain and suffering

19. Each of the following is covered by ocean marine hull insurance EXCEPT   19.____

    A. cargo strike damage   B. collision liability
    C. machinery damage   D. damage to the vessel

20. Rates for mercantile safe burglary insurance are based on each of the following factors   20.____
EXCEPT

    A. type of safe or vault
    B. territory in which risk is located
    C. extent to which safe or vault has been concealed
    D. insured's business

21. Which of the following is NOT a division of the owners', landlords', and tenants' schedule   21.____
liability policy that is essentially duplicated in a storekeepers' liability policy?

    A. Products
    B. Professional service exclusion
    C. Contractual liability
    D. Premises--operations

22. A store owner has a $10,000 blanket position bond with $20,000 excess on the cashier.   22.____
Two employees and the cashier steal a total of $65,000 from the store.
How much will be covered by the bond?

    A. $10,000   B. $30,000   C. $50,000   D. $60,000

23. A broad form personal theft policy covers damage by vandalism or malicious mischief to   23.____
a building occupied by the insured if the

    A. loss is caused to the interior of the building
    B. loss is caused during the commission of a burglary
    C. loss is not caused by a tenant
    D. building is attended by at least one custodian

24. A person who wants to self-insure for workers' compensation is required to   24.____

    A. post bonds
    B. be an employee
    C. get a permit from the state's industrial relations commission
    D. furnish proof of ability to pay compensation

25. Which of the following causes of water damage is NOT covered by a sprinkler head pol-   25.____
icy?

    A. Heat from a fire opens sprinkler head
    B. Negligent worker damages sprinkler head
    C. Defective sprinkler head opens
    D. System tank leaks water

KEY (CORRECT ANSWERS)

1.	A	11.	C
2.	B	12.	D
3.	C	13.	C
4.	D	14.	A
5.	A	15.	C
6.	D	16.	A
7.	A	17.	D
8.	B	18.	B
9.	C	19.	A
10.	A	20.	C

21. B
22. C
23. A
24. B
25. A

Glossary of Automotive Insurance Terms

I. Basic Coverages in the Typical Policy

	Payable To: Policy Holder	Other Parties
Bodily Injury Liability: Applies if the insured (the policyholder) is charged, and found legally liable for the death or injury of any other driver, passenger or pedestrian. The insurance company provides the insured's defense in a court suit, and pays any assessed judgment up to the specified limits of the policy. (Also see "Automobile Liability Insurance".) (Note: this procedure is modified in no-fault states.)	No	Yes
Medical Payments: Pays medical expenses resulting from an accident, regardless of who was at fault. Covers you and immediate family while driving, as passengers or pedestrians, as well as non-related passengers in your car.	Yes	Yes
Uninsured Motorists: Covers bodily injuries for which a hit-and-run driver or uninsured motorist is responsible. Covers you and your family as drivers, passengers or pedestrians, as well as other passengers in your car.	Yes	Yes
Property Damage Liability: Applies when your car damages another vehicle, or other property such as buildings or landscaping. Your insurer will provide your defense in the event of a court suit, and pay the assessed judgment up to the specified policy limits. (This procedure is modified in no-fault states.)	No	Yes
Comprehensive Physical Damage: Compensates for the damage to, or loss of your car from fire, theft, vandalism, water or flooding, or other specified causes other than a collision. Being made available with deductible options in many parts of the country.	Yes	No
Collision Insurance: Compensates for damage or total loss of your car due to collision with another vehicle, building or other object, regardless of who was at fault. Traditionally written with various deductible options.	Yes	No

II. General Auto Insurance Terms

Actual Cash Value: Or "ACV," the cost of repairing or replacing a vehicle. Usually defined as replacement cost less depreciation.

Automobile Liability Insurance: The insured's protection against loss due to legal fault in an accident. The maximum amount of insurance may be expressed as a single limitation, such as $50,000 (the total sum the insurer will distribute for bodily injury and property damage claims). It is also commonly expressed as a "split limit," such as 150/300/10. The first figure, representing $150,000, is the maximum payable for the injury or death of one person. The second figure, $300,000, is the limit for the total of all persons, if more than one is injured, or becomes a fatality. The third figure, for $10,000, represents the maximum to be paid for vehicle or other property damage for which the insured is liable.

Deductible Insurance: A provision, normally applied to comprehensive and collision coverage, whereby the policyholder agrees to pay a certain portion per claim. If a motorist carrying $100 deductible incurs a $500 repair bill for a damaged fender, the insurer pays $400 as settlement on the claim. Since deductibles can reduce the insurer's administrative costs for many small claims, they generally result in an overall reduced annual premium.

Financial Responsibility Laws: State laws, widely varying by degrees of enforcement, and dollar amounts, which require, or may require motorists to show proof of insurance or other form of security.

Insured: The insured is the policyholder, including other persons covered as drivers. As specified in your policy, the coverage may apply to you as the principal driver, as well as other eligible members of your family. Your policy may also cover any other person who drives your car with your permission; as well as covering you when you drive another person's car with their permission.

Loss Experience: The method by which insuring companies adjust general rates. Claims are paid out of premiums collected. If an extraordinary high amount is paid in claims during a year, rates must be increased to maintain the company's capacity to pay future claims. In general, the loss experience is based on prior three to five-year periods, which helps to produce a "leveling" effect.

Insolvency Fund: An industry system that "pitches in" to maintain the uninterrupted coverage of policyholders whose insuring company goes bankrupt. This is a rare occurrence, owing to strict financial responsibility laws for insurers, yet it is another form of protection for the policyholder.

No-Fault: Originated in 1971, and now in effect, in varying forms, in about half of all states. A system whereby, regardless of who is at fault in an accident, the insured's own company pays his or her bodily or property damages rather than bringing lawsuit against a second party. Some liability protection is still required, as when a motorist from a no-fault state travels through a non-no-fault state. The system has helped reduce premiums, but as yet it has not been uniformly successful in reducing costly court litigation. Legislation to bring no-fault to all states has been bogged down in Congress for some years.

Risk Assessment: The traditional system of computing policy cost for a new or renewal policyholder. It is based on massive statistical data on the proportionate accident rates of drivers by age, gender, marital status, community, annual mileage driven, type and age of car, and other factors. The degree of risk for each factor is well known and has been remarkably accurate over many years. Where an individual—in a composite of these factors—fits into a "higher risk" category, his or her rate tends to reduce the total rate. The individual's driving record (accidents and traffic violations, commonly within the prior three years only) is also figured into the formula.

Risk Pooling: A cooperative industry plan (somewhat similar to the insolvency fund) which makes needed insurance available to extremely "high risk" individuals. Persons with excessively frequent and costly accidents may be cancelled by their insurer and be refused insurance by most others. (If a single company carried a significant number of "high risks," their other, lower-accident customers would be penalized by higher rates, to offset a worsening loss experience.) By risk pooling, each of many companies assumes a small share of the high risk business, to thin out the detrimental effects.

State Insurance Departments: Each state has a commissioner, director or superintendent of insurance to oversee the activities of insurers licensed to operate within that state. Linked as it is to the public interest, the automobile insurance business is regulated in such areas as general practices, financial responsibility and the levels of established rates.

GLOSSARY OF BUSINESS LAW

CONTENT

	Page
abandon ---- act of god	1
administrative agency ---- antitrust acts	2
appeal ---- bill of exchange (draft)	3
bill of lading ---- circumstantial evidence	4
civil action ---- confidential relationship	5
conflict of laws ---- cy-pres doctrine	6
damages ---- disparagement of goods	7
distress for rent ---- escrow	8
estate ---- federal trade commission act	9
fellow-servant rule ---- grand jury	10
grant ---- indictment	11
inheritance ---- judgment note	12
judgment n.o.v ---- lex loci fori	13
lex loci sitae rei ---- merger of corporations	14
mesne ---- nuncupative will	15
obiter dictum ---- person	16
personal defenses ---- presumption of innocence	17
presumption of payment ---- protest	18
proximate cause ---- ratio legis	19
real defenses ---- reasale price maintenance agreement	20
rescission upon agreement ---- run with the land	21
sale of return ---- special agent	22
special damages ---- summons	23
superior servant rule ---- theory of the case	24
third-party beneficiary ---- unfair competition	25
unfair labor practice acts ---- warranties of insured	26
warranties of seller of goods ---- zoning restrictions	27

GLOSSARY OF BUSINESS LAW

A

abandon: give up or leave employment; relinquish possession of personal property with intent to disclaim title.

abate: put a stop to a nuisance; reduce or cancel a legacy because the estate of the testator is insufficient to make payment in full.

ab initio: from the beginning.

abrogate: recall or repeal; make void or inoperative.

absolute liability: liability for an act that causes harm even though the actor was not at fault.

absolute privilege: protection from liability for slander or libel given under certain circumstances to statements regardless of the fact that they are false or maliciously made.

abstract of title: history oj the transfers of title to a given piece of land, briefly stating the parties to and the effect of all deeds, wills, and judicial proceedings relating to the land.

acceleration clause: provision in a contract or any legal instrument that upon a certain event the time for the performance of specified obligations shall be advanced; for example, a provision making the balance due upon debtor's default.

acceptance: unqualified assent to the act or proposal of another; as the acceptance of a draft or bill of exchange, of an offer to make a contract, of goods delivered by the seller, or of a gift or a deed.

accession: acquisition of title to property by a person by virtue of the fact that it has been attached to property that he already owned or was the offspring of an animal he owned.

accessory after the fact: one who after the commission of a felony knowingly assists the felon.

accessory before the fact: one who is absent at the commission of the crime but who aided and abetted its commission.

accident: an event that occurs even though a reasonable man would not have foreseen its occurrence, because of which the law holds no one legally responsible for the harm caused.

accommocfa'tion party: a person who signs a commercial paper to lend credit to another.

accord and satisfaction: an agreement to substitute a different performance for that called for in the contract and the performance of that substitute agreement.

accretion: the acquisition of title to additional land when the owner's land is built up by gradual deposits made by the natural action of water.

acknowledgment: an admissioriqr confirmation, generally of an instrument and usually made before a person authorized to administer oaths, as a notary public; the purpose being to declare that the instrument was executed by the person making the instrument, or that it was his free act, or that he desires that it be recorded.

action: a proceeding brought to enforce any right.

action in personam: an action brought to impose a personal liability upon a person, such as a money judgment.

action in rem: an action brought to declare the status of a thing, such as an action to declare the title to property to be forfeited because of its illegal use.

action of assumpsit: an action brought to recover damages for breach of a contract or a quasi-contract.

action of ejectment: an action brought to recover the possession of land.

action of mandamus: an action brought to compel the performance of a ministerial or clerical act by an officer.

action of quo warranto: an action brought to challenge the authority of an officer to act or to hold office.

action of replevin: an action brought to recover the possession of personal property.

action of trespass: an action brought to recover damages for a tort.

act of bankruptcy: any of the acts specified by the national bankruptcy law which, when committed by the debtor within the four months preceding fhe filing of the petition in bankruptcy, is proper ground for declaring the debtor a bankrupt if the other requirements are met.

act of god: a natural phenomenon or act of nature that is not reasonably foreseeable.

administrative agency: a governmental commission or board given authority by statute to regulate particular matters.

administrator-administratrix: the person (man—woman) appointed to wind up and settle the estate of person who has died without a will.

adverse possession: the hostile possession of real estate, which when actual, visible, notorious, exclusive, and continued for the required number of years, will vest the title to the land in the person such adverse possession.

advisory opinion: an opinion that may be rendered in a few states when there is no actual controvers before the court and the matter is submitted by private persons or in some instances by the governor the state, to obtain the co.urt's opinion.

affidavit: a statement of facts set forth in written form and supported by the oath or affirmation of the person making the statement, setting forth that such facts are true to his knowledge or to his information ane! belief the affidavit is executed before a notary public or other person authorized to administer oaths.

affinity: the relationship that exists by virtue of marriage.

affirmative covenant: an express undertaking or promise in a deed to do an act.

agency: the relationship that exists between a person identified as a principal and another by virtue of which the latter may make contracts with third persons on behah of the principal. (Parties-principal, agent, third person)

agency coupled with an interest in the authority: an agency in which the agent has given a consideration or has paid for the right to exercise the authority granted to him.

agency coupled with an interest in the subject matter: an agency in which for a consideration the agent is given an interest in the property with which he is dealing.

agency shop: a union contract provision requiring that nonunion employees pay to the union the equivalent of union dues in order to retain their employment.

agent: one who is authorized by the principal or by operation of law to make contracts with third persor on behalf of the principal.

allonge: a paper securely fastened to a negotiable instrument in order to provide additional space· for indorsements.

alluvion: the additions made to/and by accretion.

alteration: any material change of the terms of writing made bya party thereto.

ambulatory: not effective and therefore may be changed, as in the case of a will that is not final until tl testator has died.

amicable action: an action that all parties agree should be brought and which is begun by the filing of such an agreement, rather than by serving the adverse parties with process. Although the parties agree to litigate, the dispute is real and the decision is not an advisory opinion.

amicus curiae: literally a friend of the court; one who is appointed by the court to take part in litigatior and to assist the court by furnishing his opinion in the matter.

annexation: attachment of personal property to realty in such a way as to make it become real proper and part of the realty.

annuity: a contract by which the insured pays a lump sum to the insurer and later receives fixed annu payments.

anomalous indorser: a person who signs a negotiable instrument but is not otherwise a party to the instrument.

anticipatory breach: the repudiation by a promisor of the contract prior to the time he is required to perform when such repudiation is accepted by the promisee as a breach of the contract.

anti-injunction acts: statutes prohibiting the use of injunctions in labor disputes except under exceptional circumstances; notably the federal norris-la guardia act of 1932.

anti-petrillo act: a federat statute that makes it a crime to compel a radio broadcasting station to hire musicians not needed. to pay for services not performed or to refrain from broadcasting music of school children or from foreign countries.

antitrust acts: statutes prohibiting combinations and contracts in restraint of trade, notably the federa sherman antitrust act of 1890, now generally inapplicable to labor union activity.

appeal: taking the case to a reviewing court to determine whether the judgment of the lower court or administrative agency was correct. (Parties-appellant, appellee)

appellate jurisdiction: the power of a court to hear and decide a given class of cases on appeal from another court or administrative agency.

arbitration: the settlement of disputed questions whether of law or fact, by one or more arbitrators by whose decision the parties agree to be bound. Increasingly used as a procedure for labor dispute settlement.

assignment: transfer of a right, generally used in connection with personal property rights, as rights under a contract, a negotiable instrument, an insurance policy, a mortgage, or a chattel real or lease. (parties--assignor, assignee)

assumption of risk: the common-law rule that an employee could not sue the employer for injuries caused by the ordinary risks of employment on the theory that he had assumed such risks by undertaking the work. the rule has been abolished in those areas governed by workmen's compensation laws and most employers' liability statutes.

attachment: the seizure of property of or a debt owed to, the debtor by the service of process upon a third person who is in possession of the property or who owes a debt to the debtor.

attractive nuisance doctrine: a rule imposing liability on a landowner for injuries sustained by small children playing on his land when the landowner permits a condition to exist or maintains equipment that he should realize would attract small children who could not realize the danger. The rule does not apply if an unreasonable burden would be imposed on the landowner in taking steps to protect the children.

authenticate: make or establish as genuine, official, or final, as by signing, countersigning, sealing, or any other act indicating approval.

B

bad check laws: laws making it a criminal offense to issue a bad check with intent to defraud.

baggage: such articles of necessity or personal convenience as are usually carried for personal use by passengers of common carriers.

bail: variously used in connection with the release of a person or property from the custody of the law, referring (a) to the act of releasing or bailing (b) to the persons who assume liability in the event that the released person does not appear or it is held that the property should not be released, and (c) to the bond or sum of money that such persons furnish the court or other official as indemnity for non-performance of the obligation.

bailee' lien: a specific, possessory lien of the bailee on the goods for work done to them. Commonly extended by statute to any bailee's claim for compensation and eliminating the necessity of retention of possession.

bailment: the relation that exists when personal property is delivered into the possession of another under an agreement, express or implied, that the identical property will be returned or will be delivered in accordance with the agreement. (parties-bailor, bailee)

bankruptcy: a procedure by which one unable to pay his debts may be declared a bankrupt, after which all his assets in excess of his exemption claim are surrendered to the court for administration and distribution to his creditors, and the debtor is given a discharge that releases him from the unpaid balance due on most debts.

bearer: the person in physical possession of a negotiable instrument payable to bearer.

beneficiary: the person to whom the proceeds of a life insurance policy are payable, a person for whose benefit property is held in trust, or a person given property by a will.

bequest: a gift of personal property by will.

bill of exchange (draft): an unconditional order in writing by one person upon another, signed by the person giving it, and ordering the person to whom it is directed to pay or deliver on demand or at a definite time a sum certain in money to order or to bearer.

bill of lading: a document issued by a carrier reciting the receipt of goods and the terms of the contract of transportation. Regulated by the uniform bills of lading act, the federal bills of lading act, or the uniform commercial code.

bill of sale: a writing signed by the seller reciting that he has sold to the buyer the personal property therein described.

binder: a memorandum delivered to the insured stating the essential terms of a policy to be executed in the future when it is agreed that the contract of insurance is to be effective before the written policy is executed.

blank indorsement: an indorsement that does not state to whom the instrument is to be paid.

blue-sky laws: state statutes designed to protect the public from the sale of worthless stocks and bonds

boardinghouse keeper: one regularly engaged in the business of offering living accommodations to permanent lodgers or boarders as distinguished from transient guests.

bona fide: in good faith: without any fraud or deceit.

bond: an obligation or promise in writing and sealed, generally of corporations, personal representatives trustees; fidelity bonds.

boycott: a combination of two or more persons to cause harm to another by refraining from patronizing or dealing with such other person in any way or inducing others to so refrain; commonly an incident of labor disputes.

bulk sales acts: statutes to protect creditors of a bulk seller by preventing him from obtaining cash for his goods and then leaving the state. Notice must be given creditors, and the bulk sale buyer is liable to the seller's creditors if the statute is not satisfied. Expanded to "bulk transfers" under the Code.

business trust: a form of business organization in which the owners of the property to be devoted to the business transfer the title of the property to trustees with full power to operate the business.

C

cancellation: a crossing out of a part of an instrument or a destruction of all legal effect of the instrument whether by act of party, upon breach by the other party, or pursuant to agreement or decree of court

capital: net assets of a corporation.

capital stock: the declared money value of the outstanding stock of the corporation.

cash surrender value: the sum that will be paid the insured if he surrenders his policy to the insurer.

cause of action: the right to damages or other judicial relief when a legally protected right of the plaintiff is violated by an unlawful act of the defendant.

caveat emptor: let the buyer beware. This maxim is subject to modification by warranties.

certificate of protest: a written statement by a notary public setting forth the fact that the holder had presented the negotiable instrument to the primary party on the due date and that the latter had failed to make payment.

cestui que trust: the beneficiary or person for whose benefit the property is held in trust.

charter: the grant of authority from a government to exist as a corporation. Generally replaced today by certificate approving the articles of incorporation.

chattel mortgage: a security device by which the owner of personal property transfers the title to a creditor as security for the debt owed by the owner to the creditor. Replaced under the Uniform Commercial Code by a secured transaction. (Parties-chattel mortgagor, chattel mortgagee)

chattels personal: tangible personal property.

chattels real: leases of land and buildings.

check: an order by a depositor on his bank to pay a sum of money to a payee: also defined as a bill of exchange drawn on a bank and payable on demand.

chose in action: intangible personal property in the nature of claims against another, such as a claim for accounts receivable or wages.

chose in possession: tangible personal property.

circumstantial evidence: relates to circumstances surrounding the facts in dispute from which the trier of fact may deduce what had happened.

civil action: in many states a simplified form of action combining all or many of the former common-law actions.

civil court: a court with jurisdiction to hear and determine controversies relating to private rights and duties.

closed shop: a place of employment in which only union members may beemployed. Now generally prohibited by unfair labor practice statutes.

codicil: a writing by one who has made a will which is executed with all the formality of a will and is treated as an addition to or modification of the will.

coinsurance: a clause requiring the insured to maintain insurance on his property up to a stated amount and providing that to the extent that he fails to do so the insured is to be deemed a coinsurer with the insurer so that the latter is liable only for its proportionate share of the amount of insurance required to be carried.

collateral note: a note accompanied by collateral security.

collective bargaining: the process by which the terms of employment are agreed upon through negotiations between the employer or employers within a given industry or industrial area and the union or the bargaining representative of the employees.

collective bargaining unit: the employment area within which employees are by statute authorized to select a bargaining representative, who is then to represent all the employees in bargaining collectively with the employer.

collusion: an agreement between two or more persons to defraud the government or the courts, as by obtaining a divorce by collusion when no grounds for a divorce exist, or to defraud third persons of their rights.

color of title: circumstances that make a person appear to be the owner when he in fact is not the owner, as the existence of a deed appearing to convey the property to a given person gives him color of title although the deed is worthless because it was executed by one who was not the owner of the property.

commission merchant: a bailee to whom goods are consigned for sale.

common carrier: a carrier that holds out its facilities to serve the general public for compensation without discrimination.

common law: the body of unwritten principles originally based on the usages and customs of the community which were recognized and enforced by the courts.

common stock: stock that has no right or priority over any other stock of the corporation as to dividends or distribution of assets upon dissolution.

common trust fund: a plan by which the assets of small trust estates are pooled into a common fund, each trust being given certificates representing its proportionate ownership of the fund, and the pooled fund is then invested in investments of large size.

community property: the cotenancy held by husband and wife in property acquired during their marriage under the law of some of the states, principally in the southwestern united states.

complaint: the initial pleading filed by the plaintiff in many actions which in many states may be served as original process to acquire jurisdiction over the defendant.

composition of creditors: an agreement among creditors that each shall accept a part payment as full payment in consideration of the other creditors doing the same.

concealment: the failure to volunteer information not requested.

conditional estate: an estate that will come into being upon the satisfaction of a condition precedent or that will be terminated upon the satisfaction of a condition subsequent provided in the latter case that the grantor or his heirs re-enter and retake possession of the land.

conditional sale: a credit transaction by which the buyer purchases on credit and promises to pay the purchase price in installments, while the seller retains the title to the goods, together with the right of repossession upon default, until the condition of payment in full has been satisfied. The conditional sale is replaced under the Uniform Commercial Code by a secured transaction.

confidential relationship: a relationship in which, because of the legal status of the parties or their respective physical or mental conditions or knowledge, one party places full confidence and trust in the other and relies upon him entirely for guidance.

conflict of laws: the body of law that determines the law of which state is to apply when two or more states are involved in the facts of a given case.

confusion of goods: the mixing of goods of different owners that under certain circumstances results in one of the owners becoming the owner of all the goods.

consanguinity: relationship by blood.

consideration: the promise or performance by the other party that the promisor demands as the price of his promise.

consignment: a bailment made for the purpose of sale by the bailee. (parties-consignor, consignee)

consolidation of corporations: a combining of two or more corporations in which the corporate existence of each one ceases and a new corporation is created.

constructive: an adjective employed to indicate that the noun which is modified by it does not exist but the law disposes of the matter as though it did; as a constructive bailment or a constructive trust.

contingent beneficiary: the person to whom the proceeds of a life insurance policy are payable in the event that the primary beneficiary dies before the insured.

contract: a binding agreement based upon the genuine assent of the parties, made for a lawful object, between competent parties, in the form required by law and generally supported by consideration.

contract carrier: a carrier who transports on the basis of individual contracts that it makes with each shipper, contract to sell: a contract to make a transfer of title in the future as contrasted with a present sale.

contribution: the right of a cosurety who has paid more than his proportionate share of the loss to demand that the other surety pays him the amount of the excess payment he has made.

contributory negligence: negligence of the plaintiff that contributes to his injury and at common law bars him from recovery from the defendant although the defendant may have been more negligent than the plaintiff.

conveyance: a transfer of an interest in land, ordinarily by the execution and delivery of a deed.

cooling-off period: a procedure designed to avoid strikes by requiring a specified period of delay before the strike may begin during which negotiations for a settlement must continue.

cooperative: a group of two or more persons or enterprises that act through a common agent with respect to a common objective, as buying or selling.

copyright: a grant to an author of an exclusive right to publish and sell his work for a period of 28 years renewable for a second period of 28 years.

corporation: an artificial legal person or being created by government grant, which for many purposes is treated as a natural person.

cost plus: a method of determining the purchase price or contract price by providing for the payment of an amount equal to the costs of the seller or the contractor to which is added a stated percentage as his profit.

costs: the expenses of suing or being sued, recoverable in some actions by the successful party, and in others, subject to allocation by the court. Ordinarily they do not include attorney's fees or compensation for loss of time.

counterclaim: a claim that the defendant in an action may make against the plaintiff.

covenants of title: covenants of the grantor contained in a deed that guarantee such matters as his right to make the conveyance, his ownership of the property, the freedom of the property from encumbrances, or that the grantee will not be disturbed in the quiet enjoyment of the land.

crime: a violation of the law that is punished as an offense against the state or government.

cross complaint: a claim that the defendant may make against the plaintiff.

cross-examination: the examination made of a witness by the attorney for the adverse party.

cumulative voting: a system of voting for directors in which each stockholder has as many votes as the number of voting shares he owns multiplied by the number of directors to be elected, which votes he can distribute for the various candidates as he desires.

cy-pres doctrine: the rule under which a charitable trust will be carried out as nearly as possible in the way the settlor desired, when for any reason it cannot be carried out exactly in the way or for the purposes he had expressed.

D

damages: a sum of money recovered to redress or make amends for the legal wrong or injury done.

damnum absque injuria: loss or damage without the violation of a legal right, or the mere fact that a person sustains a loss does not mean that his legal rights have been violated or that he is entitled to sue someone.

declaratory judgment: a procedure for obtaining the decision of a court on a question before any action has been taken or loss sustained. It differs from an advisory opinion in that there must be an actual, imminent controversy.

dedication: acquisition by the public or a government of title to land when it is given over by its owner to use by the public and such gift is accepted.

deed: an instrument by which the grantor (owner of land) conveys or transfers the title to a grantee.

de facto: existing in fact as distinguished from as of right, as in the case of an officer or a corporation purporting to act as such without being elected to the office or having been properly incorporated.

deficiency judgment: a personal judgment for the amount still remaining due the mortgagee after foreclosure, which is entered against any person liable on the mortgage bond. Statutes generally require the mortgagee to credit the fair value of the property against the balance due when the mortgagee has purchased the property.

del credere agent: an agent who sells goods for the principal and who guarantees to the principal that the buyer will pay for the goods.

delegation: the transfer of the power to do an act for another.

de minimis non curat lex: a maxim that the law is not concerned with trifles. Not always applied, as in the case of the encroachment of a building over the property line in which case the law will protect the landowner regardless of the extent of the encroachment.

demonstrative evidence: evidence that consists of visible, physical objects, as a sample taken from the wheat in controversy or a photograph of the subject matter involved.

demonstrative legacy: a legacy to be paid or distributed from a specified fund or property.

demurrage: a charge made by the carrier for the unreasonable detention of cars by the consignor or consignee.

demurrer: a pleading that may be filed to attack the sufficiency of the adverse party's pleading as not stating a cause of action or a defense.

dependent relative revocation: the doctrine recognized in some states that if a testator revokes or cancels a will in order to replace it with a later will, the earlier will is to be deemed revived if for any reason the later will does not take effect or no later will is executed.

deposition: the testimony of a witness taken out of court before a person authorized to administer oaths.

devise: a gift of real estate made by will.

directed verdict: a direction by the trial judge to the jury to return a verdict in favor of a specified party to the action.

directors: the persons vested with control of the corporation, subject to the elective power of the shareholders.

discharge in bankruptcy: an order of the bankruptcy court discharging the bankrupt debtor from the unpaid balance of most of the claims against him.

discharge of contract: termination of a contract by performance, agreement, impossibility, acceptance of breach, or operation of law.

discovery: procedures for ascertaining facts prior to the time of trial in order to eliminate the element of surprise in litigation.

dishonor by nonacceptance: the refusal of the drawee to accept a bill of exchange.

dishonor by nonpayment: the refusal to pay a negotiable instrument when properly presented for payment.

dismiss: a procedure to terminate an action by moving to dismiss on the ground that the plaintiff has not pleaded a cause of action entitling him to relief.

disparagement of goods: the making of malicious, false statements as to the quality of the goods of another.

distress for rent: the common-law right of the lessor to enter the premises when he was not paid the rent and to seize all personal property found on the premises. Statutes have modified or abolished this right in many states.

distributive share: the proportionate part of the estate of the decedent that will be distributed to an heir or legatee, and also as devisee in those jurisdictions in which real estate is administered as part of the decedent's estate.

domestic bill of exchange: a draft drawn in one state and payable in the same or another state.

domestic corporation: a corporation that has been incorporated by the state as opposed to incorporation by another state.

domicile: the home of a person or the state of incorporation of a corporation, to be distinguished from a place where a person lives but which he does not regard as his home, or a state in which a corporation does business but in which it was not incorporated.

dominant tenement: the tract of land that is benefited by an easement to which another tract, or servient tenement, is subject.

double indemnity: a provision for payment of double the amount specified by the insurance contract if death is caused by an accident and occurs under specified circumstances.

double jeopardy: the principle that a person who has once been placed in jeopardy by being brought to trial at which the proceedings progressed at least as far as having the jury sworn cannot thereafter be tried a second time for the same offense.

draft: see bill of exchange.

draft-varying acceptance: one in which the acceptor's agreement to pay is not exactly in conformity with the order of the instrument.

due care: the degree of care that a reasonable man would exercise to prevent the realization of harm, which under all the circumstances was reasonably forseeable in the event that such care were not taken.

due process of law: the guarantee by the 5th and 14th amendments of the federal constitution and of many state constitutions that no person shall be deprived of life, liberty, or property without due process of law, as presently interpreted, this prohibits any law either state or federal that sets up an unfair procedure or the substance of which is arbitrary or capricious.

duress: conduct that deprives the victim of his own free will and which generally gives the victim the right to set aside any transaction entered into under such circumstances.

E

easement: a permanent right that one has in the land of another, as the right to cross another's land or easement of way.

eleemosynary corporation: a corporation organized for a charitable or benevolent purpose.

embezzlement: a statutory offense consisting of the unlawful conversion of property entrusted to the wrongdoer with respect to which he owes the owner a fiduciary duty.

eminent domain: the power of a government and certain kinds of corporations to take private property against the objection of the owner provided the taking is for a public purpose and just compensation is made therefor.

encumbrance: a right held by a third person in or a lien or charge against property, as a mortgage or judgment lien on land.

equity: the body of principles that originally developed because of the inadequacy of the rules then applied by the common-law courts of England.

erosion: the loss of land through a gradual washing away by tides or currents, with the owner losing title to the lost land.

escheat: the transfer to the state of the title to a decedent's property when he dies intestate not survived by anyone capable of taking the property as his heir.

escrow: a conditional delivery of property or of a deed to a custodian or escrow holder, who in turn makes final delivery to the grantee or transferee when a specified condition has been satisfied.

estate: the extent and nature of one's interest in land. Also the assets constituting the decedent's property at the time of his death.

estate in fee simple: the largest estate possible in which the owner has the absolute and entire property in the land.

estoppel: the principle by which a person is barred from pursuing a certain course of action or of disputing the truth of certain matters when his conduct has been such that it would be unjust to permit him to do so.

evidence: that which is presented to the trier of fact as the basis on which the trier is to determine what had happened.

exception: an objection, as an exception to the admission of evidence on the ground that it was hearsy; the exclusion of particular property from the operation of a deed.

ex contractu: a claim or matter that is founded upon or arises out of a contract.

ex delicto: a claim or matter that is founded upon or arises out of a tort.

execution: the carrying out of a judgment of a court, generally directing that property owned by the defendant be sold and the proceeds first used to pay the execution or judgment creditor.

exemplary damages: damages in excess of the amount needed to compensate for the plaintiff's injury, which are awarded in order to punish the defendant for his malicious or wanton conduct so as to make an example of him.

exoneration: an agreement or provision in an agreement that one party shall not be held liable for loss; the right of the surety to demand that those primarily liable pay the claim for which the surety is secondarily liable.

expert witness: one who has acquired special knowledge in a particular field through practical experience, or study, or both, which gives him a superior knowledge so that his opinion is admissible as an aid to the trier of fact.

ex post facto law: a law making criminal an act that was lawful when done or that increases the penalty for an act which was subject to a lesser penalty when done. Such laws are generally prohibited by constitutional provisions.

extraordinary bailment: a bailment in which the bailee is subject to unusual duties and liabilities, as a hotelkeeper or common carrier

F

facility-of-payment clause: a provision commonly found in an industrial policy permitting the insurer to make payment to any member of a designated class or to any person the insurer believes equitably entitled thereto.

factor: a bailee to whom goods are consigned for sale.

factors' acts: statutes protecting persons who buy in good faith for value from a factor although the goods had not been delivered to the factor with the consent or authorization of their owner.

fair employment practice acts: statutes designed to eliminate discrimination in employment in terms of race, religion, natural origin, or sex.

fair labor standards acts: statutes, particularly the federal statute designed to prevent excessive hours of employment and low pay, the employment of young children, and other unsound practices.

fair trade acts: statutes that authorize the making of resale price maintenance agreements as to trade-mark and brand name articles, and generally provide that all persons in the industry are bound by such an agreement whether they have signed it, or not.

featherbedding: the exaction of money for services not performed or not to be performed, which is made an unfair labor practice generally and a criminal offense in connection with radio broadcasting.

federal securities act: a statute designed to protect the public from fraudulent securities.

federal securities exchange act: a statute prohibiting improper practices at and regulating security exchanges.

federal trade commission act: a statute prohibiting unfair methods of competition in interstate commerce.

fellow-servant rule: a common-law defense of the employer that barred an employee from suing an employer for injuries caused by a fellow employee.

felony: a criminal offense that is punishable by confinement in prison or by death or that is expressly stated by statute to be a felony.

financial responsibility laws: statutes that require a driver involved in an automobile accident to prove his financial responsibility in order to retain his license, which responsibility may be shown by procuring public liability insurance in a specified minimum amount.

financing factor: one who lends money to manufacturers on the security of goods to be manufactured thereafter.

firm offer: an offer stated to be held open for a specified time, which must be so held in some states even in the absence of an option contract, or under the code, with respect to merchants.

fixture: personal property that has become so attached to or adapted to real estate that it has lost its character as personal property and is part of the real estate.

food, drug, and cosmetic act: a federal statute prohibiting the interstate shipment of misbranded or adulterated foods, drugs, cosmetics, and therapeutic devices.

forbearance: refraining from doing an act.

foreclosure: procedure for enforcing a mortgage resulting in the public sale of the mortgaged property and less commonly in merely barring the right of the mortgagor to redeem the property from the mortgage.

foreign (international) bill of exchange: a bill of exchange made in one nation and payable in another

foreign corporation: a corporation incorporated under the laws of another state.

forgery: the fraudulent making or altering of an instrument that apparently creates or alters a legal liability of another.

fraud: the making of a false statement of a past or existing fact with knowledge of its falsity or with reckless indifference as to its truth with the intent to cause another to rely thereon, and he does rely thereon to his injury.

freight forwarder: one who contracts to have goods transported and, in turn, contracts with carriers for such transportation.

fructus industriales: crops that are annually planted and raised.

fructus naturales: fruits from trees, bushes, and grasses growing from perennial roots.

fungible goods: goods of a homogenous nature of which any unit is the equivalent of any other unit or is treated as such by mercantile usage.

future advance mortgage: a mortgage given to secure additional loans to be made in the future as well as an original loan.

G

garnishment: the name given in some states to attachment proceedings.

general creditor: a creditor who has a claim against the debtor but does not have any lien on any of the debtor's property, whether as security for his debt or by way of a judgment or execution upon a judgment.

general damages: damages that in the ordinary course of events follow naturally and probably from the injury caused by the defendant.

general legacy: a legacy to be paid out of the assets generally of the testator without specifying any particular fund or source from which the payment is to be made.

general partnenhip: a partnership in which the partners conduct as co-owners a business for profit, and each partner has a right to take part in the management of the business and has unlimited liability.

gift causa mortis: a gift made by the donor because he believed he faced immediate and impending death, which gift is revoked or is revocable under certain circumstances.

grace period: a period generally of 30 or 31 days after the due date of a premium of life insurance in which the premium may be paid.

grand jury: a jury not exceeding 23 in number that considers evidence of the commission of crime and prepares indictments to bring offenders to trial before a petty jury.

grant: convey real property; an instrument by which such property has been conveyed, particularly in the case of a government.

gratuitous bailment: a bailment in which the bailee does not receive any compensation or advantage.

grievance settlement: the adjustment of disputes relating to the administration or application of existing contracts as compared with disputes over new terms of employment.

guarantor: one who undertakes the obligation of guaranty.

guaranty: an undertaking to pay the debt of another if the creditor first sues the debtor and is unable to recover the debt from the debtor or principal. (In some instances the liability is primary, in which case it is the same as suretyship.)

H

hearsay evidence: statements made out of court which are offered in court as proof of the information contained in the statements, which, subject to many exceptions, are not admissible in evidence.

hedging: the making of simultaneous contracts to purchase and to sell a particular commodity at a future date with the intention that the loss on one transaction will be offset by the gain on the other.

heirs: those persons specified by statute to receive the estate of a decedent that he has not disposed by will.

holder: the person in possession of a negotiable instrument payable to him as payee or indorsee, or the person in possession of a negotiable instrument payable to bearer.

holder in due course: the holder of a negotiable instrument under such circumstances that he is treated as favored and is given immunity from certain defenses.

holder through a holder in due course: a person who is not himself a holder in due course but is a holder of the instrument after it was held by some prior party who was a holder in due course, and who is given the same rights as a holder in due course.

holographic will: a will written by the testator in his own hand.

hotelkeeper: one regularly engaged in the business of offering living accommodations to all transient persons.

hung jury: a petty jury that has been unable to agree upon a verdict.

I

ignorantia legis non excusat: ignorance of the law is not an excuse.

implied contract: a contract expressed by conduct or implied or deduced from the facts. Also used to refer to a quasi-contract.

imputed: vicariously attributed to or charged to another, as the knowledge of an agent obtained while acting in the scope of his authority is imputed to his principal.

incidental authority: authority of an agent that is reasonably necessary to execute his express authority.

incontestable dause: a provision that after the lapse of a specified time the insurer cannot dispute the policy on the ground of misrepresentation or fraud of the insured or similar wrongful conduct.

in custodia legis: in the custody of the law.

indemnity: the right of a person secondarily liable to require that a person primarily liable pay him for his loss when the secondary party discharges the obligation which the primary party should have discharged; the right of an agent to be paid the amount of any loss or damage sustained by him without his fault because of his obedience to the principal's instructions; an undertaking by one person for a consideration to pay another person a sum of money to indemnify him when he incurs a specified loss.

independent contractor: a contractor who undertakes to perform a specified task according to the terms of a contract but over whom the other contracting party has no control except as provided for by the contract.

indictment: a formal accusation of crime made by a grand jury which accusation is then tried by a petty or trial jury.

inheritance: the estate which passes from the decedent to his heirs.

injunction: an order of a court of equity to refrain from doing (negative injunction) or to do (affirmative or mandatory injunction) a specified act. Its use in labor disputes has been greatly restricted by statute.

in pari delicto: equally guilty; used in reference to a transaction as to which relief will not be granted to either party because both are equally guilty of wrongdoing.

insolvency: an excess of debts and liabilities over assets.

insurable interest: an interest in the non occurrence of the risk insured against, generally because such occurrence would cause financial loss, although sometimes merely because of the close relationship between the insured and the beneficiary.

insurance: a plan of security against risks by charging the loss against a fund created by the payments made by policyholders.

intangible personal property: an interest in an enterprise, such as an interest in a partnership or stock of a corporation, and claims against other persons, whether based on contract or tort.

interlineation: a writing between the lines or adding to the provisions of a document, the effect thereof depending upon the nature of the document.

interlocutory: an intermediate step or preceding that does not make a final disposition of the action and from which ordinarily no appeal may be taken.

international bill of exchange: an instrument made in one nation and payable in another.

interpleader: a form of action or proceeding by which a person against whom conflicting claims are made may bring the claimants into court to litigate their claims between themselves, as in the case of a bailor when two persons each claim to be the owner of the bailed property, or an insurer when two persons each claim to be the beneficiary of the insurance policy.

inter se: among or between themselves, as the rights of partners inter se or as between themselves.

inter vivos: any transaction which takes place between living persons and creates rights prior to the death of any of them.

intestate: the condition of dying without a will as to any property.

intestate succession: the distribution made as directed by statute of property owned by the decedent of which he did not effectively dispose by will.

ipso facto: by the very act or fact in itself without any further action by anyone.

irrebuttable presumption: a presumption which cannot be rebutted by proving that the facts are to the contrary; not a true presumption but merely a rule of law described in terms of a presumption.

irreparable injury to property: an injury that would be of such a nature or inflicted upon such an interest that it would not be reasonably possible to compensate the injured party by the payment of money damages because the property in question could not be purchased in the open market with the money damages which the defendant could be required to pay.

J

joint and several contract: a contract in which two or more persons are jointly and severally obligated or are jointly and severally entitled to recover.

joint contract: a contract in which two or more persons is jointly liable or jointly entitled to performance under the contract.

joint stock company: an association in which the shares of the members are transferable and control is delegated to a group or board.

joint tenancy: the estate held by two or more jointly with the right of survivorship as between them, unless modified by statute.

joint venture: a relationship in which two or more persons combine their labor or property for a single undertaking and share profits and losses equally unless otherwise agreed.

judgment: the final sentence, order, or decision entered into at the conclusion of the action.

judgment note: a promissory note containing a clause authorizing the holder of the note to enter judgment against the maker of the note if it is not paid when due. Also called cognovit note.

judgment n.o.v.: a judgment which may be entered after verdict upon the motion of the losing party on the ground that the verdict is so wrong that a judgment should be entered the opposite of the verdict, or nonobstante veredicto (notwithstanding the verdict).
judgment on the pleadings: a judgment which may be entered after all the pleadings are filed when it is clear from the pleadings that a particular party is entitled to win the action without proceeding any further.
judicial sale: a sale made under order of court by an officer appointed to make the sale or by an officer having such authority as incident to his office. The sale may have the effect of divesting liens on the property.
jurisdiction: the power of a court to hear and determine a given class of cases; the power to act over a particular defendant.
jurisdictional dispute: a dispute between rival labor unions which may take the form of each claiming that particular work should be assigned to it.
justifiable abandonment by employee: the right of an employee to abandon his employment because of nonpayment of wages, wrongful assault, and the demand for the performance of services not contemplated or injurious working-conditions.
justifiable discharge of employee: the right of an employer to discharge an employee for nonperformance of duties, fraud, disobedience, disloyalty, or incompetence.

L

laches: the rule that the enforcement of equitable rights will be denied when the party has delayed so long that rights of third persons have intervened or the death or disappearance of witnesses would prejudice any party through the loss of evidence.
land: earth, including all things imbedded in or attached thereto, whether naturally or by act of man.
last clear chance: the rule that if the defendant had the last clear chance to have avoided injuring the plaintiff, he is liable even though the plaintiff had also been contributorily negligent. In some states also called the humanitarian doctrine.
law of the case: matters decided in the course of litigation which are binding on the parties in the subsequent phases of the litigation.
leading questions: questions which suggest the desired answer to the witness, or assume the existence of a fact which is in dispute.
lease: an agreement between the owner of property and a tenant by which the former agrees to give possession of the property to the latter in consideration of the payment of rent. (parties-landlord or lessor, tenant or lessee)
leasehold: the estate or interest which the tenant has in land rented to him.
legacy: a gift of personal property made by will.
legal tender: such form of money as the law recognizes as lawful and declares that a tender thereof in the proper amount is a proper tender which the creditor cannot refuse.
letters of administration: the written authorization given to an administrator as evidence of his appointment and authority.
letters testamentary: the written authorization given to an executor as evidence of his appointment and authority.
levy: a seizure of property by an officer of the court in execution of a judgment of the court, although in many states it is sufficient if the officer is physically in the presence of the property and announces the fact that he is "seizing" it, although he then allows the property to remain where he found it.
lex loci: the law of the place where the material facts occurred as governing the rights and liabilities of the parties.
lex loci contractus: the law of the place where the contract was made as governing the rights and liability of the parties to a contract with respect to certain matters.
lex loci fori: the law of the state in which the action is brought as determining the rules of procedure applicable to the action.

lex loci sitae rei: the law of the place where land is located as determining the validity of acts done relating thereto.
libel: the defamation of another without legal justification.
license: a personal privilege to do some act or series of acts upon the land of another not amounting to an easement or a right of possession, as the placing of a sign thereon.
lien: a claim or right against property existing by virtue of the entry of a judgment against its owner or by the entry of a judgment and a levy thereunder on the property, or because of the relationship of the claimant to the particular property, such as an unpaid seller.
life estate: an estate for the duration of a life.
limited jurisdiction: a court with power to hear and determine cases within certain restricted categories
limited liability: loss of contributed capital as maximum liability.
limited partnership: a partnership in which at least one partner has a liability limited to the loss of the capital contribution that he has made to the partnership, and such a partner neither takes part in the management of the partnership nor appears to the public to be a partner.
lineal consanguinity: the relationship that exists when one person is a direct descendant from the other
liquidated damages: a provision stipulating the amount of damages to be paid in event of default or breach of contract.
liquidation: the process of converting property into money whether of particular items of property or all the assets of a business.
lis pendens: the doctrine that certain types of pending actions are notice to everyone so that if any right is acquired from a party to that action, the transferee takes that right subject to the outcome of the pending action.
lobbying contract (illegal): a contract by which one party agrees to attempt to influence the action of a legislature or congress, or any members thereof, by improper means.
lottery: any plan by which a consideration is given for a chance to win a prize.
lucri causa: with the motive of obtaining gain or pecuniary advantage.

M

majority: of age, as contrasted with being a minor; more than half of any group, as a majority of stockholders.
malice in fact: an intention to injure or cause harm.
malice in law: a presumed intention to injure or cause harm when there is no privilege or right to do the act in question, which presumption cannot be contradicted or rebutted.
maliciously inducing breach of contract: the wrong of inducing an employee to break his contract with his employer or inducing the breach of any other kind of contract with knowledge of its existence and without justification.
malum in se: an offense that is criminal because contrary to the fundamental sense of a civilized community, as murder.
malum prohibitum: an offense that is criminal not because inherently wrong but is prohibited for the convenience of society, as overtime parking.
marshalling assets: the distribution of a debtor's assets in such a way as to give the greatest benefit to all of his creditors.
martial law: government exercised by a military commander over property and persons not in the armed forces, as contrasted with military law which governs the military personnel.
mechanics' lien: protection afforded by statute to various types of laborers and persons supplying materials, by giving them a lien on the building and land that has been improved or added to by them
mens rea: the mental state that must accompany an act to make the act a crime, sometimes described as the "guilty mind," although appreciation of guilt is not required.
merger by judgment: the discharge of a contract through being merged into a judgment which is entered in a suit on the contract.
merger of corporations: a combining of corporations by which one absorbs the other and continues to exist, preserving its original charter and identity while the other corporation ceases to exist.

mesne: intermediate, intervening, as mesne profits, which are the fruits or income from the land received in between the time that the true owner was wrongfully dispossessed and the time that he recovers the land.

misdemeanor: a criminal offense which is neither treason nor a felony.

misrepresentation: a false statement of fact although made innocently without any intent to deceive.

mobilia sequuntur personam: the maxim that personal property follows the owner and in the eyes of the law is located at the owner's domicile.

moratorium: a temporary suspension by statute of the enforcement of debts or the foreclosure of mortgages.

mortgage: an interest in land given by the owner to his creditor as security for the payment to the creditor of a debt, the nature of the interest depending upon the law of the state where the land is located. (Parties--mortgagor, mortgagee)

multiple insurers: insurers who agree to divide a risk so that each is only liable for a specified portion.

N

National Labor Management Relations Act: the federal statute, also known as the taft-hartley act, designed to protect the organizational rights of labor and to prevent unfair labor practices by management or labor.

natural and probable consequences: those ordinary consequences of an act which a reasonable man would foresee.

negative covenant: an undertaking in a deed to refrain from doing an act.

negligence: the failure to exercise due care under the circumstances in consequence of which harm is proximately caused to one to whom the defendant owed a duty to exercise due care.

negligence per se: an action which is regarded as so improper that it is declared by law to be negligent in itself without regard to whether due care was otherwise exercised.

negotiable instruments: drafts or bills of exchange, promissory notes, checks, and certificates of deposit in such form that greater rights may be acquired thereunder than by taking an assignment of a contract right.

negotiation: the transfer of a negotiable instrument by indorsement and delivery by the person to whom then payable in the case of order paper, and by physical transfer in the case of bearer paper.

nominal damages: a nominal sum awarded the plaintiff in order to establish that his legal rights have been violated although he in fact has not sustanied any actual loss or damages.

nominal partner: a person who in fact is not a partner but who holds himself out as a partner or permits others to do so.

Norris-Laguardia Anti-Injunction Act: a federal statute prohibiting the use of the injunction in labor disputes, except in particular cases.

notice of dishonor: notice given to parties secondarily liable that the primary party to the instrument has refused to accept the instrument or to make payment when it was properly presented for that purpose.

novation: the discharge of a contract between two parties by their agreeing with a third person that such third person shall be substituted for one of the original parties to the contract, who shall thereupon be released.

nudum pactum: a mere promise for which there is no consideration given and which therefore is ordinarily not enforceable.

nuisance: any conduct that harms or prejudices another in the use of his land or which harms or prejudices the public.

nuisance per se: an activity which is in itself a nuisance regardless of the time and place involved.

nuncupative will: an oral will made and declared by the testator in the presence of witnesses to be his will and generally made during the testator's last illness.

O

obiter dictum: that which is said in the opinion of a court in passing or by the way, but which is not necessary to the determination of the case and is therefore not regarded as authoritative as though it were actually involved in the decision.

obliteration: any erasing, writing upon or crossing out that makes all or part of a will impossible to read and which has the effect of revoking such part when done by the testator with the intent of effecting a revocation.

occupation: taking and holding possession of property; a method of acquiring title to personal property which has been abandoned.

open-end mortgage: a mortgage given to secure additional loans to be made in the future as well as the original loan.

operation of law: the attaching of certain consequences to certain facts because of legal principles that operate automatically, as contrasted with consequences which arise because of the voluntary actions of a party designed to create those consequences.

opinion evidence: evidence not of what the witness himself observed but the conclusion which he draws from what he observed, or in the case of an expert witness, also from what he is asked or what he has heard at the trial.

option contract: a contract to hold an offer to make a contract open for a fixed period of time.

P

paper title: the title of a person evidenced only by deeds or matter appearing of record under the recording statutes.

parol evidence rule: the rule that prohibits the introduction in evidence of oral or written statements made prior to or contemporaneously with the execution of a complete written contract, deed, or instrument, in the absence of clear proof of fraud, accident, or mistake causing the omission of the statement in question.

passive trust: a trust that is created without imposing any duty to be performed by the trustee and is therefore treated as an absolute transfer of the title to the trust beneficiary.

past consideration: something that has been performed in the past and which therefore cannot be consideration for a promise made in the present.

PATENT: the grant to an inventor of an exclusive right to make and sell his invention for a nonrenewable period of 17 years: a deed to land given by a government to a private person.

pawn: a pledge of tangible personal property rather than of documents representing property rights.

pecuniary legacy: a general legacy of a specified amount of money without indicating the source from which payment is to be made.

per autre vie: limitation of an estate. An estate held by A during the lifetime of B, is an estate of A per autre vie.

per curiam opinion: an opinion written "by the court" rather than by a named judge when all the judges of the court are so agreed on the matter that it is not deemed to merit any discussion and may be simply disposed of.

perpetual succession: a phrase describing the continuing life of the corporation unaffected by the death of any stockholder or the transfer by stockholders of their stock.

perpetuities, rule against: a rule of law that prohibits the creation of an interest in property which will not become definite or vested until a date further away than 21 years after the death of persons alive at the time the owner of the property attempts to create the interest.

per se: in, through, or by itself

person: a term that includes both natural persons, or living people, and artificial persons, as corporations which are created by act of government.

personal defenses: limited defenses that cannot be asserted by the defendant against a holder in due course or a holder through a holder in due course. This term is not expressly used in the Uniform Commercial Code.

per stirpes: according to the root or by way of representation. Distribution among heirs related to the decedent in different degrees, the property being divided into lines of descent from the decedent and the share of each line then divided within the line by way of representation.

petty jury: the trial jury of twelve. Also petit jury.

picketing: the placing of persons outside of places of employment or distribution so that by words or banners they may inform the public of the existence of a labor dispute.

pleadings: the papers filed by the parties in an action in order to set forth the facts and frame the issues to be tried, although under some systems, the pleadings merely give notice or a general indication of the nature of the issues.

pledge: a bailment given as security for the payment of a debt or the performance of an obligation owed to the pledgee. (Parties-pledgor. pledgee)

police power: the power to govern; the power to adopt laws for the protection of the public health, welfare, safety, and morals.

policy: the paper evidencing the contract of insurance.

polling the jury: the process of inquiring of each juror individually in open court as to whether the verdict announced by the foreman of the jury was agreed to by him.

possession: exclusive domain and control of property.

possessory lien: a right to retain possession of property of another as security for some debt or obligation owed the lienor which right continues only as long as possession is retained.

possibility of reverter: the nature of the interest held by the grantor after conveying land outright but subject to a condition or provision that may cause the grantee's interest to become forfeited and the interest to revert to the grantor of his heirs.

postdate: to insert or place a later date on an instrument than the actual date on which it was executed.

power of appointment: a power given to another, commonly a beneficiary of a trust, to designate or appoint who shall be beneficiary or receive the fund upon his death.

power of attorney: a written authorization to an agent by the principal.

precatory words: words indicating merely a desire or a wish that another use property for a particular purpose but which in law will not be enforced in the absence of an express declaration that the property shall be used for the specified purpose.

pre-emptive offer of shares: the right, subject to many exceptions, that each shareholder has that whenever the capital stock of the corporation is increased he will be allowed to subscribe to such a percentage of the new shares as his old shares bore to the former total capital stock.

preferred creditor: a creditor who by some statute is given the right to be paid first or before other creditors.

preferred stock: stock that has a priority or preference as to payment of dividends or upon liquidation, or both.

preponderance of evidence: the degree or quantum of evidence in favor of the existence of a certain fact when from a review of all the evidence it appears more probable that the fact exists than that it does not. The actual number of witnesses involved is not material nor is the fact that the margin of probability is very slight.

prescription: the acquisition of a right to use the land of another. as an easement, through the making of hostile, visible and notorious use of the land, continuing for the period specified by the local law.

presumption: a rule of proof which permits the existence of a fact to be assumed from the proof that another fact exists when there is a logical relationship between the two or when the means of disproving the assumed fact are more readily within the control or knowledge of the adverse party against whom the presumption operates.

presumption of death: the rebuttable presumption which arises that a person has died when he has been continuously absent and unheard of for a period of 7 years.

presumption of innocence: the presumption of fact that a person accused of crime is innocent until it is shown that he in fact is guilty of the offense charged.

presumption of payment: a rebuttable presumption that one performing continuing services which would normally be paid periodically, as weekly or monthly, has in fact been paid when a number of years have passed without any objection or demand for payment having been made.

presumptive heir: a person who would be the heir if the ancestor should die at that moment.

pretrial conference: a conference held prior to the trial at which the court and the attorneys seek to simplify the issues in controversy and eliminate matters not in dispute.

price: the consideration for a sale of goods.

prima facie: such evidence as by itself would establish the claim or defense of the party if the evidence were believed.

primary beneficiary: the person designated as the first one to receive the proceeds of a life insurance policy, as distinguished from a contingent beneficiary who will receive the proceeds only if the primary beneficiary dies before the insured.

primary liability: the liability of a person whose act or omission gave rise to the cause of action and who in all fairness should therefore be the one to pay the victim of his wrong, even though others may also be liable for his misconduct.

principal: one who employs an agent to act on his behalf; the person who as between himself and the surety is primarily liable to the third person or creditor.

principal in the first degree: one who actually engages in the commission or perpetration of a crime.

principal in the second degree: one who is actually or constructivey present at the commission of the crime and who aids and abets in its commission.

private carrier: a carrier owned by the shipper, such as a company's own fleet of trucks.

privileged communication: information which the witness may refuse to testify to because of the relationship with the person furnishing the information, as husband-wife, attorney-client.

privilege from arrest: the immunity from arrest of parties, witnesses, and attorneys while present within the jurisdiction for the purpose of taking part in other litigation.

privity: a succession or chain of relationship to the same thing or right, as a privity of contract, privity of estate, privity of possession.

probate: the procedure for formally establishing or proving that a given writing is the last will and testament of the person purporting to have signed it.

process: a writ or order of court generally used as a means of acquiring jurisdiction over the person of the defendant by serving him with process.

profit a prendre: the right to take a part of the soil or produce of the land of another, such as to take timber or water.

promissory estoppel: the doctrine that a promise will be enforced although not supported by consideration when the promisor should have reasonably expected that his promise would induce action or forebearance of a definite and substantial character on the part of the promisee, and injustice can only be avoided by enforcement of the promise.

promissory note: an unconditional promise in writing made by one person to another, signed by the maker, engaging to pay on demand, or at a definite time, a sum certain in money to order or to bearer (Parties-maker, payee)

promissory representation: a representation made by the applicant to the insurer as to what is to occur in the future.

promissory warranty: a representation made by the applicant to the insurer as to what is to occur in the future which the applicant warrants will occur.

promoters: the persons who plan the formation of the corporation and sell or promote the idea to others

proof: the probative effect of the evidence: the conclusion drawn from the evidence as to the existence of particular facts.

property: the rights and interests one has in anything subject to ownership.

pro rata: proportionately, or divided according to a rate or standard.

protest: the formal certification by a notary public or other authorized person that proper presentment of a commercial paper was made to the primary party and that he defaulted, the certificate commonly also including a recital that notice was given to secondary parties.

proximate cause: the act which is the natural and reasonably foreseeable cause of the harm or event which occurs and injures the plaintiff.

proximate damages: damages which in the ordinary course of events are the natural and reasonably foreseeable result of the defendant's violation of the plaintiff's rights.

proxy: a written authorization by a stockholder to another person to vote the stock owned by the stockholder; the person who is the holder of such a written authorization.

public charge: a person who because of a personal disability or lack of means of support is dependent upon public charity or relief for sustenance.

public domain: public or government owned lands.

public easement: a right of way for use by members of the public at large.

public policy: certain objectives relating to health, morals, and integrity of government that the law seeks to advance by declaring invalid any contract which conflicts with those objectives even though there is no statute expressly declaring such contract illegal.

punitive damages: damages in excess of those required to compensate the plaintiff for the wrong done, which are imposed in order to punish the defendant because of the particularly wanton or willful character of his wrongdoing.

purchase-money mortgage: a mortgage given by the purchaser of land to the seller to secure the seller for the payment of the unpaid balance of the purchase price, which the seller purports to lend the purchaser.

purchaser in good faith: a person who purchases without any notice or knowledge of any defect of title, misconduct, or defense.

Q

qualified acceptance: an acceptance of a draft that varies the order of the bill in some way.

qualified indorsement: an indorsement that includes words such as "without recourse" evidencing the intent of the indorser that he shall not be held liable for the failure of the primary party to pay the instrument.

quantum meruit: an action brought for the value of the services rendered the defendant when there was no express contract as to the payment to be made.

quantum valebant: an action brought for the value of goods sold the defendant when there was no express contract as to the purchase price.

quasi: as if, as though it were, having the characteristics of; a modifier employed to indicate that the subject is to be treated as though it were in fact the noun which follows the word "quasi:" as in quasi contract, quasi corporation, quasi public corporation.

quid pro quo: literally "what for what." An early form of the concept of consideration by which an action for debt could not be brought unless the defendant had obtained something in return for his obligation.

quitclaim deed: a deed by which the grantor purports only to give up whatever right or title he may have in the property without specifying or warranting that he is transferring any particular interest.

quorum: the minimum number of persons, shares represented, or directors who must be present at a meeting in order that business may be lawfully transacted.

R

ratification by minor: the approval of a contract given by a minor after attaining majority.

ratification of agency: the approval of the unauthorized act of an agent or of a person who is not an agent for any purpose after the act has been done, which has the same effect as though the act had been authorized before it was done.

ratio decidendi: the reason or basis for deciding the case in a particular way.

ratio legis: the reason for a principle or rule of law.

real defenses: certain defenses (universal) that are available against any holder of a negotiable instrument regardless of his character, although this term is not expressly used by the Uniform Commercial Code.

real evidence: tangible objects that are presented in the courtroom for the observation of the trier of fact as proof of the facts in dispute or in support of the theory of a party.

real property: land and all rights in land.

reasonable care: the degree of care that a reasonable man would take under all the circumstances then known.

rebate: a refund made by the seller or the carrier of part of the purchase price or freight bill. Generally illegal as an unfair method of competition.

rebuttable presumption: a presumption which may be overcome or rebutted by proof that the actual facts were different than those presumed.

receiver: an impartial person appointed by a court to take possession of and manage property for the protection of all concerned.

recognizance: an obligation entered into before a court to do some act, such as to appear at a later date for a hearing. Also called a contract of record.

redemption: the buying back of one's property, which has been sold because of a default, upon paying the amount which had been originally due together with interest and costs.

referee: an impartial person selected by the parties or appointed by a court to determine facts or decide matters in dispute.

referee in bankruptcy: a referee appointed by a bankruptcy court to hear and determine various matters relating to bankruptcy proceedings.

reformation: a remedy by which a written instrument is corrected when it fails to express the actual intent of both parties because of fraud, accident, or mistake.

registration of titles: a system generally known as the Torrens system of permanent registration of titles to all land within the state.

reimbursement: the right of one paying money on behalf of another which such other person should have himself paid to recover the amount of the payment from him.

release of liens: an agreement or instrument by which the holder of a lien on property, such as a **mortgage lien**, releases the property from the lien although the debt itself is not released.

remedy: the action or procedure that is followed in order to enforce a right or to obtain damages for injury to a right.

remote damages: damages which were in fact caused by the defendant's act but the possibility that such damages should occur seemed so improbable and unlikely to a reasonable man that the law does not impose liability for such damages.

renunciation of duty: the repudiation of one's contractual duty in advance of the time for performance, which repudiation may be accepted by the adverse party as an anticipatory breach.

renunciation of right: the surrender of a right or privilege as the right to act as administrator or the right to receive a legacy under the will of a decedent.

reorganization of corporation: procedure devised to restore insolvent corporations to financial stability through readjustment of debt and capital structure either under the supervision of a court of equity or of bankruptcy.

repossession: any taking again of possession although generally used in connection with the act of a conditional vendor in taking back the property upon the default of the conditional vendee.

representations: statements, whether oral or written, made to give the insurer the information which it needs in writing the insurance, and which if false and relating to a material fact will entitle the insurer to avoid the contract.

representative capacity: action taken by one not on his own behalf but on behalf of another, as an executor acting on behalf of the decedent's estate, or action taken both on one's behalf and on behalf of others, as a stockholder bringing a representative action.

resale price maintenance agreement: an agreement that the buyer will not resell a trademark or brand name article below a stated minimum price which agreement, by virtue of fair trade laws, is valid not only as between the contracting parties but may also bind other persons in the trade who know of the agreement although they did not sign it.

rescission upon agreement: the setting aside of a contract by the action of the parties as though the contract had never been made.

rescission upon breach: the action ot one party to a contract to set the contract aside when the other party is guilty of a breach of the contract.

reservation: the creation by the grantor of a right that did not exist before, which he reserves or keeps for himself upon making a conveyance of property.

residuary estate: the balance of the testator's estate available for distribution after all administrative expenses, exemptions, debts, taxes, and specific, pecuniary, and demonstrative legacies have been paid.

res inter alios acta: the rule that transactions and declarations between strangers having no connection with the pending action are not admissible in evidence.

res ipsa loquitur: the rebuttable presumption that the thing speaks for itself when the circumstances are such that ordinarily the plaintiff could not have been injured had the defendant not been at fault.

res judicata: the principle that once a final judgment is entered in an action between the parties, it is binding upon them and the matters cannot be litigated again by bringing a second action.

respondeat superior: the doctrine that the principal or employer is vicariously liable for the unauthorized torts committed by his agent or employee while acting with the scope of his agency or the course of his employment, respectively.

restraints on alienation: limitations on the ability of the owner to convey freely as he chooses. Such limitations are generally regarded as invalid.

restrictive covenants: covenants in a deed by which the grantee agrees to refrain from doing specified acts.

restrictive indorsement: an indorsement that prohibits the further transfer, constitutes the indorsee the agent of the indorser, vests the title in the indorsee in trust for or to the use of some other person, is conditional, or is for collection or deposit.

resulting trust: a trust that is created by implication of law when the purpose of the original trust fails or is fully performed and the cy pres doctrine is inapplicable, the effect of the resulting trust being to revert the remaining property to the settlor or his heirs.

retaliatory statute: a statute that provides that when a corporation of another state enters the state it shall be subject to the same taxes and restrictions as would be imposed upon a corporation from the retaliating state if it had entered the other state. Also called reciprocity statutes.

reversible error: an error or defect in court proceedings of so serious a nature that on appeal the appellate court will set aside the proceedings of the lower court.

reversionary interest: the interest that a lessor has in property which is subject to an outstanding lease.

revival of judgment: the taking of appropriate action to preserve a judgment, in most instances to continue the lien of the judgment that would otherwise expire after a specified number of years.

revival of will: the restoration by the testator of a will which he had previously revoked.

rider: a slip of paper executed by the insurer and intended to be attached to the insurance policy for the purpose of changing it in some respect.

riparian rights: the right of a person through whose land runs a natural watercourse to use the water free from unreasonable pollution or diversion by the upper riparian owners and from blocking by lower riparian owners.

risk: the peril or contingency against which the insured is protected by the contract of insurance.

Robinson-Patman Act: a federal statute designed to eliminate price discrimination in interstate commerce.

run with the land: the concept that certain covenants in a deed to land are deemed to "run" or pass with the land so that whoever owns the land is bound by or entitled to the benefit of the covenants.

S

sale or return: a sale in which the title to the property passes to the buyer at the time of the transaction but he is given the option of returning the property and restoring the title to the seller.

scienter: knowledge, referring to those wrongs or crimes which require a knowledge of wrong in order to constitute the offense.

scope of employment: the area within which the employee is authorized to act with the consequence that a tort committed while so acting imposes liability upon the employer.

seal: at common law an impression on wax or other tenacious material attached to the instrument. Under modern law, any mark not ordinarily part of the signature is a seal when so intended, including the letters "L. S." and the word "seal," or a pictorial representation of a seal, without regard to whether the had been printed or typed on the instrument before its signing.

sealed verdict: a verdict that is rendered when the jury returns to the courtroom during an adjournment of the court, the verdict then being written down and sealed and later affirmed before the court when the court is in session.

seaman's will: an oral or informal written will made by a seaman to dispose of his personal property.

secondary evidence: copies of original writings or testimony as to the contents of such writings which are admissible when the original cannot be produced and the inability to do so is reasonably explained.

secret partner: a partner who takes an active part in the management of the partnership but is not known to the public as a partner.

secured transaction: a sale of goods on credit that provides some form of special protection for the seller.

settlor: one who settles property in trust or creates a trust estate.

severable contract: a contract the terms of which are such that one part may be separated or severed from the other, so that a default as to one part is not necessarily a default as to the entire contract.

several contracts: separate or independent contracts made by different persons undertaking to perform the same obligation.

severalty: sole ownership of property by one person.

severed realty: real property that has been cut off and made moveable, as by cutting down a tree, and which thereby loses its character as real property and becomes personal property.

shareholder's action: an action brought by one or more shareholders on behalf of the shareholders generally and of the corporation to enforce a cause of action of the corporation against third persons.

sheriff's deed: the deed executed and delivered by the sheriff to the purchaser at a sale conducted by the sheriff in his official capacity.

Sherman Antitrust Act: a federal statute prohibiting combinations and contracts in restraint of interstate trade, now generally inapplicable to labor union activity.

shop right: the right of an employer to use in his business without charge an invention discovered by an employee during working hours and with the employer's material and equipment.

sight draft: a draft or bill of exchange payable on sight or when presented for payment.

silent partner: a partner who takes no active part in the business without regard to whether he is known to the public as a partner.

sitdown strike: a strike in which the employees remain in the plant and refuse to allow the employer to operate it.

slander: defamation of character by spoken words or gestures.

slander of title: the malicious making of false statements as to a seller's title.

slander per se: certain words deemed slanderous without requiring proof of damages to the victim, as words charging a crime involving moral turpitude and an infamous punishment, a disease which would exclude from society, or which tend to injure the victim in his business, profession, or occupation.

slowdown: a slowing down of production by employees without actual stopping of work.

social security acts: siatutes providing for assistance for the aged, blind, unemployed, and similar classes of persons in need.

soldier's will: an oral or informal written will made by a soldier to dispose of his personal estate.

special agent: an agent authorized to transact a specific transaction or to do a specific act.

special damages: damages that do not necessarily result from the injury to the plaintiff but at the same time are not so remote that the defendant should not be held liable therefore provided that the claim for special damages is properly made in the action.

special indorsement: an indorsement that specifies the person to whom the instrument is indorsed.

special jurisdiction: a court with power to hear and determine cases within certain restricted categories.

specific (identified) goods: goods which are so identified to the contract that no other goods may be delivered in performance of the contract.

specific lien: the right of a creditor to hold particular property or assert a lien on any particular property of the debtor because of the creditor's having done work on or having some other association with the property, as distinguished from having a lien generally against the assets of the debtor merely because the debtor is indebted to him.

specific performance: an action brought to compel the adverse party to perform his contract on the theory that merely suing him for damages for its breach will not be an adequate remedy.

spendthrift trust: a trust, which to varying degrees, provides that creditors of the beneficiary shall not be able to reach the principal of income held by the trustee and that the beneficiary shall not be able to assign his interest in the trust.

spoliation: an alteration or change made to a written instrument by a person who has no relationship to or interest in the writing. It has no effect as long as the terms of the instrument can still be ascertained.

stare decisis: the principle that the decision of a court should serve as a guide or precedent and control the decision of a similar case in the future.

status quo: the requirement that before a contract may be rescinded, the status quo must be restored, that is, the parties must be placed in their original positions prior to the making of the contract.

Statute of Frauds: a statute, which in order to prevent fraud through the use of perjured testimony, requires that certain types of transactions be evidenced in writing in order to be binding or enforceable.

Statute of limitations: a statute that restricts the period of time within which an action may be brought.

stoppage in transitu: the right of the unpaid seller to stop goods being shipped to the buyer while they are still in transit and to recover them when the buyer becomes insolvent.

stop payment: an order by a depositor to his bank to refuse to make payment of his check when presented for payment.

sublease: a transfer of the premises by the lessee to a third person. The sublessee or subtenant, for a period less than the term of the original lease.

subpoena: a court order directing a person to appear as a witness. In some states also it is the original process that is to be served on the defendant in order to give the court jurisdiction over his person.

subpoena duces tecum: a court order directing a person to appear as a witness and to bring with him specified relevant papers.

subrogation: the right of a party secondarily liable to stand in the place of the creditor after he has made payment to the creditor and to enforce the creditor's right against the party primarily liable in order to obtain indemnity from him.

subsidiary corporation: a corporation that is controlled by another corporation through the ownership by the latter of a controlling amount of the voting stock of the former.

subsidiary term: a provision of a contract that is not fundamental or does not go to the root of the contract.

substantial performance: the equitable doctrine that a contractor substantially performing a contract in good faith is entitled to recover the contract price less damages for noncompletion or defective work.

substantive law: the law that defines rights and liabilities.

substitution: discharge of contracts by substituting another in its place.

subtenant: one who rents the leased premises from the original tenant for a period of time less than the balance of the lease to the original tenant.

sui generis: in a class by itself, or its own kind.

sui juris: legally competent, possessing capacity.

summary judgment: a judgment entered by the court when no substantial dispute of fact is present, the court acting on the basis of affidavits which show that the claim or defense of a party is a sham.

summons: a writ by which an action was commenced under the common law.

superior servant rule: an exception to the fellow-servant rule that is made when the injured servant is under the control of the servant whose conduct caused him injury.

supersedeas: a stay of proceedings pending the taking of an appeal or an order entered for the purpose of effecting such a stay.

surcharge: a money judgment entered against a fiduciary for the amount of loss which his negligence or misconduct has caused the estate under his control.

suretyship: an undertaking to pay the debt or be liable for the default of another.

surrender: the yielding up of the tenant's leasehold estate to the lessor in consequence of which the lease terminates.

survival acts: statutes which provide that causes of action shall not terminate on death but shall survive and may be enforced by or against a decedent's estate.

survivorship: the right by which a surviving joint tenant or tenant by the entireties acquires the interest of the predeceasing tenant automatically upon his death.

symbolic delivery: the delivery of goods by delivery of the means of control, as a key or relevant document of title, as a negotiable bill of lading.

syndicate: an association of individuals formed to conduct a particular business transaction, generally of a financial nature.

T

tacking: the adding together of successive periods of adverse possession of persons in privity with each other in order to constitute a sufficient period of continuous adverse possession to vest title thereby.

Taft-Hartley Act: popular name for the National Labor Management Relations Act of 1947,

tenancy at sufferance: the holding over by a tenant after his lease has expired of the rented land without the permission of the landlord and prior to the time that the landlord has elected to treat him as a trespasser or a tenant.

tenancy at will: the holding of land for an indefinite period that may be terminated at any time by the landlord or by the landlord and tenant acting together.

tenancy for years: a tenancy for a fixed period of time, even though the time is less than a year.

tenancy from year to year: a tenancy which continues indefinitely from year to year until terminated.

tenancy in common: the relation that exists when two or more persons own undivided interests in property.

tenancy in partnership: the ownership relation that exists between partners under the Uniform Partnership Act.

tender of payment: an unconditional offer to pay the exact amount of money due at the time and place specified by the contract.

tender of performance: an unconditional offer to perform at the time and in the manner specified by the contract.

tentative trust: a trust which arises when money is deposited in a bank account in the name of the depositor "in trust for" a named person.

terminable fee: an estate that terminates upon the happening of a contingency without any entry by the grantor or his heirs, as a conveyance for "so long as" the land is used for a specified purpose.

testamentary: designed to take effect at death, as by disposing of property or appointing an executor.

testate: the condition of leaving a will upon death.

testate succession: the distribution of an estate in accordance with the will of the decedent.

testator-testatrix: a man-woman who makes a will.

testimonium clause: a concluding paragraph in a deed, contract, or other instrument, reciting that the instrument has been executed on a specified date by the parties.

testimony: the answers of witnesses under oath to questions given at the time of the trial in the presence of the trier of fact.

theory of the case: the rule that when a case is tried on the basis of one theory, the appellant in taking an appeal cannot argue a different theory to the appellate court.

third-party beneficiary: a third person whom the parties to a contract intend to benefit by the making of the contract and to confer upon him the right to sue for breach of the contract.
tie-in sale: the requirement imposed by the seller that the buyer of particular goods or equipment also purchase certain other goods from the seller in order to obtain the original property desired.
time draft: a bill of exchange payable at a stated time after sight or a stated time after a certain date.
title insurance: a form of insurance by which the insurer insures the buyer of real property against the risk of loss should the title acquired from the seller be defective in any way.
toll the statute: stop the running of the period of the Statute of Limitations by the doing of some act by the debtor.
Torrens System: see registration of titles.
tort: a private injury or wrong arising from a breach of a duty created by law.
trade acceptance: a draft or bill of exchange drawn by the seller of goods on the purchaser at the time of sale and accepted by the purchaser.
trade fixtures: articles of personal property which have been attached to the freehold by a tenant and which are used for or are necessary to the carrying on of the tenant's trade.
trade-mark: a name, device, or symbol used by a manufacturer or seller to distinguish his goods from those of other persons.
trade name: a name under which a business is carried on and, if fictitious, it must be registered.
trade secrets: secrets of any character peculiar and important to the business of the employer that have been communicated to the employee in the course of confidential employment.
treason: an attempt to overthrow or betray the government to which one owes allegiance.
treasury stock: stock of the corporation which the corporation has reacquired.
trier of fact: in most cases a jury, although it may be the judge alone in certain classes of cases, as in equity, or in any case when jury trial is waived, or an administrative agency or commission.
trust: a transfer of property by one person to another with the understanding or declaration that such property be held for the benefit of another, or the holding of property by the owner in trust for another, upon his declaration of trust, without a transfer to another person. (Parties—settlor, trustee, beneficiary.)
trust corpus: the fund or property that is transferred to the trustee as the body or subject matter of the trust.
trust deed: a form of deed which transfers the trust property to the trustee for the purposes therein stated, particularly used as a form of mortgage when the trustee is to hold the title to the mortgagor's land in trust for the benefit of the mortgage bondholders.
trustee de son tort: a person who is not a trustee but who has wrongly intermeddled with property of another and rather than proceed against him for the tort, the law will require him to account for the property as though he were such a trustee.
trustee in bankruptcy: an impartial person elected to administer the bankrupt's estate.
trust receipt: a credit security device under which the wholesale buyer executes a receipt stating that he holds the purchased goods in trust for the person financing the purchase by lending him money. The trust receipt is replaced by the secured transaction under the Uniform Commercial Code.

U

uberrima fides: utmost good faith, a duty to exercise the utmost good faith which arises in certain relationships, as that between an insurer and the applicant for insurance.
ultra vires: an act or contract which the corporation does not have authority to do or make. Glossary
underwriter: an insurer.
undisclosed principal: a principal on whose behalf an agent acts without disclosing to the third person the fact that he is an agent nor the identity of the principal.
undue influence: the influence that is asserted upon another person by one who dominates that person.
unfair competition: the wrong of employing competitive methods that have been declared unfair by statute or an administrative agency.

unfair labor practice acts: statutes that prohibit certain labor practices and declare them to be unfair labor practices.

unincorporated association: a combination of two or more persons for the furtherance of a common nonprofit purpose.

union contract: a contract between a labor union and an employer or group of employers prescribing the general terms of employment of workers by the latter.

union shop: under present unfair labor practice statutes, a place of employment where nonunion men may be employed for a trial period of not more than 30 days after which the nonunion worker must join the union or be discharged.

universal agent: an agent authorized by the principal to do all acts that can lawfully be delegated to a representative.

usury: the lending of money at greater than the maximum rate allowed by law.

V

vacation of judgment: the setting aside of a judgment.

valid: legal.

verdict: the decision of the trial or petty jury.

vice-principal rule: the rule that persons performing supervisory functions or acting as vice employers are not to be regarded as fellow servants of those under their authority for the purpose of determining the liability of the employer for the injuries of the employee at common law.

void: no legal effect and not binding on anyone.

voidable: a transaction that may be set aside by one party thereto because of fraud or similar reason but which is binding on the other party until the injured party elects to avoid the contract.

voidable preference: a preference given by the bankrupt to one of his creditors, but which may be set aside by the trustee in bankruptcy.

voir dire examination: the preliminary examination of a juror or a witness to ascertain that he is qualified to act as such.

volenti non fit injuria: the maxim that the defendant's act cannot constitute a tort if the plaintiff had consented thereto.

voluntary nonsuit: a means of the plaintiff's stopping a trial at any time by moving for a voluntary nonsuit.

voting trust: the transfer by two or more persons of their shares of stock of a corporation to a trustee who is to vote the shares and act for such shareholders.

W

waiver: the release or relinquishment of a known right or objection.

warehouse receipt: a receipt issued by the warehouseman for goods stored with him. Regulated generally by the Uniform Warehouse Receipts Act or the Uniform Commercial Code, which clothe the receipt with some degree of negotiability.

warehouseman: a person regularly engaged in the business of storing the goods of others for compensation. If he holds himself out to serve the public without discrimination, he is a public warehouseman.

warranties of indorser of negotiable instrument: the implied covenants made by an indorser of a negotiable instrument distinct from any undertaking to pay upon the default of the primary party.

warranties of insured: statements or promises made by the applicant for insurance which he guarantees to be as stated and which if false will entitle the insurer to avoid the contract of insurance in many jurisdictions.

warranties of seller of goods: warranties consisting of express warranties that relate to matters forming part of the basis of the bargain; warranties as to title and right to sell; and the implied warranties which the law adds to a sale depending upon the nature of the transaction.

warranty deed: a deed by which the grantor conveys a specific estate or interest to the grantee and covenants that he has transferred the estate or interest by making one or more of the covenants of title.

warranty of authority: an implied warranty of an agent that he has the authority which he purports to possess.

warranty of principal: an implied warranty of an agent that he is acting for an existing principal who has capacity to contract.

watered stock: stock issued by a corporation as fully paid when in fact it is not.

way: an easement to pass over the land of another.

will: an instrument executed with the formality required by law, by which a person makes a disposition of his property to take effect upon his death or appoints an executor.

willful: intentional as distinguished from accidental or involuntary. In penal statutes, with evil intent or legal malice, or without reasonable ground for believing one's act to be lawful.

witness: a person who has observed the facts to which he testifies or an expert witness who may testify on the basis of observation, the testimony presented in the court, or hypothetical questions put to him by the attorneys in the case.

Wool Products Labeling Act: a federal statute prohibiting the misbranding of woolen fabrics.

workmen's compensation: a system providing for payments to workmen because they have been injured from a risk arising out of the course of their employment while they were employed at their employment or have contracted an occupational disease in that manner, payment being made without consideration of the negligence of any party.

works of charity: in connection with Sunday laws, acts involved in religious worship or aiding persons in distress.

works of necessity: in connection with Sunday laws, acts that must be done at the particular time in order to be effective in saving life, health, or property.

Y

year and a day: the common-law requirement that death result within a year and a day in order to impose criminal liability for homicide.

Z

zoning restrictions: restrictions imposed by government on the use of property for the advancement of the general welfare.

www.ingramcontent.com/pod-product-compliance
Lightning Source LLC
Chambersburg PA
CBHW081826300426
44116CB00014B/2495